MARGARET THATCHER

THATCHER

 ON

LEADERSHIP

MARGARET THATCHER

THATCHER

ON

LEADERSHIP

LESSONS FOR
AMERICAN CONSERVATIVES TODAY

NILE GARDINER
AND STEPHEN THOMPSON

Since 1947
REGNERY
Publishing, Inc.
An Eagle Publishing Company • Washington, DC

Cataloging-in-Publication data on file with the Library of Congress
ISBN 978-1-62157-164-3

Published in the United States by
Regnery Publishing, Inc.
One Massachusetts Avenue NW
Washington, DC 20001
www.Regnery.com

Manufactured in the United States of America
10 9 8 7 6 5 4 3 2 1

Books are available in quantity for promotional or premium use. Write to Director of Special Sales, Regnery Publishing, Inc., One Massachusetts Avenue NW, Washington, DC 20001, for information on discounts and terms, or call (202) 216-0600.

Distributed to the trade by
Perseus Distribution
250 West 57th Street
New York, NY 10107

To the Iron Lady.
A fearless warrior for freedom.

CONTENTS

WHY MARGARET THATCHER'S LEADERSHIP MATTERS TODAY

"We believe that individuals have a right to liberty that no state can take away. That government is the servant of the people, not its master."
—MARGARET THATCHER, SPEECH TO CONSERVATIVE PARTY CONFERENCE, OCTOBER 14, 1988[1]

The reelection of Barack Obama left American conservatives as close to despair as they had been in decades. Those are precisely the circumstances in which the leadership of Margaret Thatcher is most instructive and inspiring.

Obama's America and 1970s Britain

The parallels between the United States under Barack Obama and the Great Britain of 1979 are striking. Thatcher took the helm of a country that was economically moribund, internationally inert, and utterly demoralized. If anything, the challenges she faced were even greater than those faced by American conservatives today. Decades of socialist rule had created a society where dependency on government was chronic. The welfare state, engineered by the Labour government that came in after the Second World War, was all-consuming and vastly expensive. It was the enemy of free enterprise, and it fostered an anti-capitalist culture, reinforced by powerful public-sector unions. The government was bloated, hugely bureaucratic, and ineffective. Small government conservatism had been largely written off, even by much of the leadership of the Conservative Party itself. Britain's ruling elites were convinced that the country was in irreversible decline.

After she overcame tremendous obstacles to become the leader of the Conservative Party in 1975, Margaret Thatcher outlined a conservative agenda for retaking power that challenged the ideology of socialism, rejected big government, and stood for economic liberty. She rejected the idea that Britain's best days were behind it. She offered a relentlessly optimistic vision of the future, giving hope to millions of Britons who wished to enjoy the fruits of a capitalist economy and improve their circumstances.

Upon becoming prime minister, Thatcher embarked on the biggest downsizing of government in modern British history, privatizing large state-owned industries and utilities. Her government sold off large numbers of council homes (public housing), allowing millions of Britons to own their own homes for the first time. In addition, millions more bought shares in privatized companies, giving them a stake in Britain's economic revival. At the same time, she took an axe to government spending, reined in the national debt, cut taxes, and revitalized the City of London, all with an emphasis upon reducing the role of the state and encouraging individual responsibility.

The economic revival at home was matched by robust British leadership abroad. Thatcher restored British military capabilities and aggressively fought terrorism. Her cultivation of the reformist Mikhail Gorbachev, while stiffening the backbone of the West in confronting communism, was vital to the downfall of the Soviet empire.

There Is Still Hope for America

Margaret Thatcher, like Ronald Reagan, demonstrated why principled conservative leadership works. Liberalism reigns in the White House, but America remains a conservative nation at heart. Polls have consistently shown that conservatism is the leading ideology in the United States, with conservatives outnumbering liberals by an almost two-to-one margin.[2]

Not only is America an ideologically conservative country but it also benefits from a remarkably strong conservative movement, from the big think tanks of Washington to thousands of grassroots organizations that campaign for limited government. American conservatism is strengthened by Fox News and by talk radio, with hugely popular hosts such as Rush Limbaugh, Sean Hannity, Mark Levin, and Laura Ingraham. The most widely read national newspaper is the *Wall Street Journal*, with a higher daily circulation than the *New York Times*.[3] It is no coincidence that the largest national political gathering of the year[4] is the Conservative Political Action Conference (CPAC), which draws in several thousand conservative activists to its annual meeting in Washington, D.C.

America's Conservatives Must Lead

Margaret Thatcher succeeded because she understood the concerns of the conservative grassroots on core issues such as the economy, government spending, and taxes. She won over millions more to the conservative cause not by watering down her message or shifting her positions but by presenting an attractive vision of economic freedom. Thatcher won over large numbers of voters by winning the war of ideas and encouraging them to join her approach—she did not seek to adapt herself to their image.

American conservatives should take heart from those extraordinary political victories and be inspired by her loyalty to conservative ideals. American conservatives must be the champions of small government, free enterprise, and individual freedom. In her speech to the Conservative Party conference in 1988, Thatcher conveyed a message that is relevant to the United States today: "We believe that individuals have a right to liberty that no state can take away. That Government is the servant of the people, not its master. That the role of Government is to strengthen our freedom, not deny it. That the economic role of Government is to establish a climate in which enterprise can flourish, not to elbow enterprise out of the way."[5]

Margaret Thatcher always believed in American leadership. Americans should believe in it too.

CHAPTER ONE

THE
IRON LADY

"I do not believe that history is writ clear and unchallengeable. It doesn't just happen. History is made by people: its movement depends on small currents as well as great tides, on ideas, perceptions, will and courage, the ability to sense a trend, the will to act on understanding and intuition."
—MARGARET THATCHER, "THE NEW RENAISSANCE,"
SPEECH TO THE ZURICH ECONOMIC SOCIETY,
MARCH 14, 1977[1]

Farewell to a Champion of Liberty

In St. Paul's Cathedral on April 17, 2013, Great Britain mourned its first woman prime minister with the most solemn and splendid funeral for a politician since Winston Churchill's in 1965. The world leaders in attendance included a former vice president and three secretaries of state from America, Lech Walesa of Poland, and F. W. de Klerk, the South African president who brought the apartheid era to an end. Tens of thousands of her countrymen lined the streets for her funeral procession, and millions more watched on television. Nearly a quarter century after her political career had ended, Margaret Thatcher could still command the attention of a country whose decline she had refused to accept: "For we believed passionately that decline and surrender were just not good enough for Britain. We were confident that the values of the British people, their work ethic, their love of freedom and sense of natural justice could once more be harnessed to promote liberty and make Britain more prosperous and more influential."[2]

A Speech That Shaped History

The leader laid to rest that day in the cemetery of the Royal Hospital Chelsea was known to friend and foe as the "Iron Lady," a title bestowed on her in 1976, three years before she became prime minister, by a Russian army officer and journalist. The Tory leader had delivered a speech titled "Britain Awake" at Kensington Town Hall, forcefully warning of the danger the Soviet Union posed to her country and the West. Yury Gavrilov reported on the speech for the newspaper *Krasnaya Zvezda* ("Red Star").

Struck by her determined tone, Gavrilov wanted to compare Thatcher to Otto von Bismarck, the "Iron Chancellor" who unified Germany, so he dubbed her the "Iron Lady."

"It was my idea," Gavrilov told a British newspaper in 2007. "I didn't go to anyone higher up. I put those two words in a headline on January 24, 1976. At the time it seemed that everyone liked the label. Her opponents thought it reflected her stubbornness and inflexibility. But her supporters took it as a sign of strength."[3]

Old Soviet leaders, schooled in the murderous politics of communism, had contempt for what Lenin called "useful idiots"—those in the West who believed they were working for peace, but were merely doing the bidding of the Soviet Union. Gavrilov saw immediately that Thatcher would be no useful idiot: "… I did have the feeling that the Soviet Union would soon face a tough opponent. She would not be bullied into endless talks about peace and friendship, she would ignore the anti-war movement in Britain and she would also be a strong ally to the U.S."[4]

Though Gavrilov was impressed by the speech, Russian leaders were upset and protested. Thatcher recalled that a "stream of crude invective flowed from the different Soviet propaganda organs."[5] The reaction in Moscow to the "Iron Lady" speech foreshadowed the hostile response to President Ronald Reagan's "Evil Empire" speech seven years later, when he famously predicted that the Soviet Union would collapse. Gavrilov recalled that until the Iron Lady speech, "Soviet cartoonists had portrayed Britain as a toothless lion. But after my headline and despite our countries' not very good relations and the ideological confrontation, Thatcher was always respected in the USSR."[6]

Thatcher delivered that speech at the height of 1970s détente, when there was a supposed "thaw" in the Cold War between the West and the Soviet Union after nearly three decades of a divided Europe, conflict in Asia, and fears of nuclear war. Many in the West naively thought an end to the Cold War was in sight. Some were even revising history, saying the Soviet Union was not so bad after all. The thinking behind détente was that Communist and democratic countries could coexist in peace and mutual respect. Large defense budgets, the Left supposed, were no longer necessary. "The Socialists [in Britain], in fact, seem to regard defence as almost infinitely cuttable," Thatcher cautioned. "If there are further cuts, perhaps the Defence Secretary should change his title, for the sake of accuracy, to the Secretary for Insecurity."[7]

"The Russians are bent on world dominance," Thatcher declared, "and they are rapidly acquiring the means to become the most powerful imperial nation the world has seen."[8] The Soviet Union was increasing its military spending, she warned, and seizing every opportunity to expand communism after decades of containment. Communism was spreading in Southeast Asia in the wake of the Vietnam War, and decolonization and civil war were creating opportunities for Communist insurgents in Mozambique, Angola, and elsewhere in Africa. In Europe, Portugal and Italy were in danger of falling to the Communists through the ballot box.

"Euro-communism," it was imagined, could be democratic, different from the totalitarianism of the Soviet Union.

By 1976, Margaret Thatcher and Ronald Reagan were challenging détente, warning that the West faced grave danger if it did not strengthen its defenses and fight the spread of communism. At best, détente bought the West time before the final push against the Soviet Union under Reagan and Thatcher in the 1980s. It achieved modest success in the hands of clear-eyed leaders like Richard Nixon and Henry Kissinger, but the strategy required a toughness that few Western leaders possessed. As practiced by the naïve and posturing President Jimmy Carter and other liberal and socialist leaders after 1976, détente came to be viewed as a sign of weakness in Moscow. The Russians were convinced that they faced an adversary with no stomach for the fight. Carter, after all, worried about Americans' "inordinate fear of communism." As he hugged and kissed the Kremlin bosses, he assured them, "We want to be friends with the Soviets."[9]

The Soviet response was to become more aggressive and brutal around the world, invading Afghanistan and supporting Communist dictatorships and guerilla movements in Central America, expanding its geopolitical reach beyond anything imagined in the days of Stalin. Russian archives opened since the collapse of the Soviet Union have revealed that the Communists in Moscow and their global allies feared Western strength and clinically took advantage of any weakness. The old heirs of Stalin thought they had the upper hand in the 1970s, but their confidence was shaken by the ascent of Margaret Thatcher and Ronald Reagan.

In her Iron Lady speech, Thatcher posed some devastating questions: "Has détente induced the Russians to cut back on their defence programme? Has it dissuaded them from brazen intervention in Angola? Has it led to any improvement in the conditions of Soviet citizens, or the subject populations of Eastern Europe? We know the answers." Surveying the record of Soviet aggression around the globe, she insisted, "We must remember that there are no Queensberry rules in the contest that is now going on. And the Russians are playing to win."[10] These were fighting words, strikingly different from the usual naïve rhetoric the Soviet leaders were used to hearing at the height of détente. They preferred to be kissed and hugged by Jimmy Carter.

The young army officer reporting for the *Krasnaya Zvezda* newspaper was insightful. Among other things, Gavrilov concluded that Thatcher would not be "bullied" by the Soviets. This was a leader. Like Reagan, she recognized that the Soviet Union was a failure: "They know that they are a super power in only one sense—the military sense," she said. "They are a failure in human and economic terms."[11] Communists in Moscow were quickly learning that they would face a formidable opponent if Thatcher became prime minister. And it worried them, for they knew, better than many intelligence agencies around the world, that their system was also doomed to fail. But the end of Communist dominance was still fifteen years away, and very few leaders other than Margaret Thatcher and Ronald Reagan could see beyond détente.

Thatcher reacted to her new moniker of the Iron Lady with a mixture of amusement and pride: "I quickly saw that they had inadvertently put me on a pedestal as their strongest European opponent."[12]

A week after *Krasnaya Zvezda*'s "Iron Lady" headline, Thatcher addressed some 250 fellow Conservatives at a formal dinner in her constituency of Finchley, London. Her remarks revealed her ultimate pleasure with the new nickname, for it could be used as a weapon for freedom:

> I stand before you tonight in my Red Star chiffon evening gown. [Laughter, Applause], my face softly made up and my fair hair gently waved [Laughter], the Iron Lady of the Western world. A cold war warrior, an amazon philistine, even a Peking plotter. Well, am I any of these things?

("No!"….)

Well yes, if that's how they … [Laughter]. Yes I am an iron lady, after all it wasn't a bad thing to be an iron duke [as Wellington was known], yes if that's how they wish to interpret my defence of values and freedoms fundamental to our way of life.[13]

Margaret Thatcher's courage and conviction would soon lead her to 10 Downing Street, where she would stay for eleven years. Her enemies feared her. Her supporters worshipped her. Her country warmed to her. And the world began to take note of a new kind of British leader.

"The Greatest Conservative of All Time"

On April 19, 1979, two weeks before the election that would make her prime minister, Margaret Thatcher addressed a rally in Birmingham. Buffeted by inflation, unemployment, crime, and union unrest, Britain was being called the "sick man of Europe." Thatcher appealed for the revival of a great nation, rejecting Dean Acheson's infamous 1962 jibe that Britain "has lost an empire and has not yet found a role." Nowhere in the world had the values of democracy and civilization been "more treasured, more jealously guarded, more subtly protected than on this island of ours," she reminded her audience.

I believe that those who read our destiny this way are utterly and profoundly wrong. They understand neither why we acquired our Empire, nor why we disengaged from our Imperial responsibilities with a skill and a readiness which no Empire in history ever showed before. We remain as we always have been, a force for freedom, muted, even weakened these last few years, but still with the fires burning deep within us, ready to be kindled and go forward again.

This is the difference between us and the other imperial powers in our history books. Our vitality comes not from our possessions but from our unquenchable belief in freedom, and that is why, whatever lies ahead, we shall be there. We shall always be there in the forefront of the struggle to resist tyranny and to hold freedom high. This is our heritage and our destiny. For that heritage and for that destiny we Conservatives have always stood. Let us not forsake it now.[14]

The Conservatives' rivals in 1979 were the Labour and Liberal Parties, which had ruled in a coalition government under Labour's James Callaghan until the previous summer. Notable for the backroom deals that held it together, the "Lib-Lab" pact had prolonged Britain's economic decline. "The experiences of the last two or three years have been utterly abhorrent," Thatcher declared. "It reduced the whole standard of public life and Parliamentary democracy to a series of wheels and deals."[15] Known as "Sunny Jim" for his easygoing manner, Callaghan was actually a wily politician. He was personally popular with the British public, but the mood of the country had changed dramatically by 1979. Britain was desperate for strong leadership after five years of socialist failure.

Thatcher reminded her audience in Birmingham, "The Russians said that I was an Iron Lady. They were right. Britain needs an Iron Lady."[16] British voters agreed. On May 3, 1979, the Conservative Party captured a majority of seats in the House of Commons. The next day Margaret Thatcher was summoned to Buckingham Palace, where the Queen asked her to form a government.

Victory in 1979 would be the first of three for the Conservatives with Thatcher at the helm, triumphs that define modern British history. The reason for these victories was simple—Margaret Thatcher was one of the greatest leaders of modern times. At the Conservative Party conference in 2008, Tory MPs and party activists voted her "the greatest Conservative of all time," ahead of Winston Churchill, Edmund Burke, Lord Salisbury, and Benjamin Disraeli—the Mount Rushmore of British Conservative statesmen.[17]

No Conservative leader since the 1820s has matched Thatcher's record of winning elections. Her hat trick of electoral victories in 1979, 1983, and 1987 would make her the longest continuously serving prime minister since Lord Liverpool (1812–1827). A fourth Tory victory in 1992, after Thatcher had left office, still belonged to her. For John Major, her successor as prime minister, benefited from her eleven years of leadership in the same way that George H. W. Bush benefited in 1988 from Ronald Reagan's eight years of leadership. Since its defeat to Labour in 1997, the Conservative Party has had no fewer than four leaders, only one of whom, David Cameron, has become prime minister.

Among Thatcher's twentieth-century Conservative predecessors—Arthur Balfour, Bonar Law, Stanley Baldwin, Neville Chamberlain, Winston Churchill, Anthony Eden, Harold Macmillan, Alec Douglas-Home, Edward Heath—only Churchill rivals her in appeal among Tories. And while some British surveys rank Churchill above Thatcher as the country's greatest twentieth-century leader, his popularity never translated into comparable electoral success.

After presiding over victory during World War II, Churchill and the Conservative Party were heavily defeated by Clement Attlee and the Labour Party in July 1945, against the backdrop of a Europe that lay in ruins. It was a stunning loss, leading to six years of Labour rule that laid the foundations for socialism and the modern welfare state in Britain. It was the beginning of a new era of big government for Britain, one that would lead ultimately to national decline in the 1970s and the deadly stranglehold of socialism over the British people. It took a conservative revolution led by the Iron Lady to break the grip of socialism, a revolution that was to turn Britain once again into a world power and an economic powerhouse. Thirty years after Churchill's defeat, a new set of ideas based on traditional conservative values emerged, changing Britain forever. Thatcherism, not socialism, would be the dominant ideology in Britain in the 1980s.

CHAPTER TWO

THATCHERISM

*"Prosperity will not come by inventing more and more lavish
public expenditure programmes. You do not grow richer by ordering
another cheque-book from the bank. No nation ever grew more
prosperous by taxing its citizens beyond their capacity to pay."*
—MARGARET THATCHER, SPEECH TO CONSERVATIVE PARTY
CONFERENCE, OCTOBER 14, 1983[1]

How Thatcherism Changed British Politics

It was billed as "the ultimate Eighties revival night" by the London *Times*—a 650-plus gathering on October 13, 2005, of the *Who's Who* of Britain in the 1980s to celebrate the eightieth birthday of Margaret Thatcher. Guests included the Queen and Prince Philip. Even the Labour prime minister, Tony Blair, was there with his wife. A younger generation of Conservatives were also in attendance, those who had admired Thatcher at school and university and later tried to follow her example in public life. The guest of honor, however, was late: she had to take a call from President George W. Bush.

The assembled well-wishers had often had their differences in the 1980s—and still do—but on this night they joined to celebrate the life of Margaret Thatcher. One of her fiercest critics inside the Conservative Party, Lord Howe of Aberavon, was there. The former foreign secretary and chancellor of the exchequer conceded that "her real triumph was to have transformed not just one party but two, so that when Labour did eventually return, the great bulk of Thatcherism was accepted as irreversible."[2]

Tony Blair's presence at the celebration demonstrated the truth of Howe's praise. He had presided over an urgent modernization of the Labour Party, even abandoning the party constitution's infamous commitment to state socialism. Blair also maintained Thatcher's restrictions on trade unions and did not try to reverse her privatizations of major industries. When Labour returned to power after eighteen years, it was not James Callaghan's party.

In 1994 Margaret Thatcher had attended another birthday party, this one for Ronald Reagan, his eighty-third. It was one of the last times these two twentieth-century giants appeared in public together. Reagan told the large gathering in Washington that night that he had recently watched President Bill Clinton's State of the Union speech. "I'm reminded of the old adage that imitation is the sincerest form of flattery. Only in this case, it's not flattery, but grand larceny—the intellectual theft of ideas that you and I recognize as our own."[3] As Thatcher laughed with the rest of the audience, she must have known that the Labour Party was committing the same "crime" back home.

Thatcher and Thatcherism

Several twentieth-century Tory prime ministers received knighthoods and peerages, but only Margaret Thatcher got an "ism" named after her. That distinction is one of the ironies of history because she generally despised "isms." In 1997, Thatcher returned to Washington to unveil a portrait of herself and Ronald Reagan—*A Shared Vision* by Mark Balma—standing on the South Portico of the White House looking out toward the National Mall. She talked on that occasion about the twentieth-century struggle between freedom and the terrible "isms" that had troubled so much of modern history. She added that Communism, Nazism, and "most of the bad isms have come from Germany.... Fascism from the rest of the continent of Europe."[4]

The critique of "isms" was a constant theme. On receiving an honorary degree from Tel Aviv University in 1986, Thatcher said, "I must assure you that as a newly appointed Doctor of Philosophy I do not intend to retire to an Ivory Tower. Or devote the rest of my life to some learned treatise on Thatcherism. Or indeed any other 'ism'. They so quickly become 'wasms.'"[5]

Fourteen years later at New York's Hofstra University, Thatcher announced that she never intended for an "ism" to be affixed to her name. In fact, she considered the modern attachment to "isms" to be contrary to her political philosophy. "Starting with the French Revolution, and then greatly encouraged by the Bolshevik Revolution," she said, "modern times have been plagued by 'isms,' that is by ideologies, in effect secular religions. Most of them were unrelievedly bad." Focusing on socialism, she surveyed the damage caused by collectivist ideologies. "Communism accounted for approaching a hundred million deaths. It enslaved the East, while its first cousin socialism impoverished much of the West. Nazism—that other brand of socialism—and its tamer forbear Fascism killed about 25 million. All have left scars on our societies which perhaps will never fully heal," she added.[6] Thatcherism, of course, is not a typical "ism"—an all-encompassing ideology like socialism or communism, a utopian doctrine that does not expand freedom but kills it. "About one thing though, I would like to be clear," she insisted. "I don't regard Thatcherism as an 'ism' in any of these senses. And if I ever invented an ideology, that certainly wasn't my intention."[7]

The Tenets of Thatcherism

Despite her reservations about "isms," "Thatcherism" swiftly became a household term. It was only after she left office that Thatcher herself attempted formally to define the "principles of Thatcherism." She did this in early September 1992 in speeches delivered in Taiwan and South Korea.

Thatcher called herself a "Conservative revolutionary,"[8] which at first glance seems like a contradiction in terms. But sometimes to "conserve," one must restore or rebuild what has been destroyed. As she explained to her Asian audiences,

> It is a well-known fact that restoring values or institutions which are weakened or entirely lost requires a very different approach from just conserving or strengthening them. In a world, or a country, in which Socialism has not yet done its destructive worst you may be able to get away with mere pragmatism.
>
> But when the storm has wreaked havoc, uprooting social structures and distorting economic impulses, a more fundamental reconstruction is called for. That in turn requires the formulation, exposition and implementation of principles.
>
> As a Conservative revolutionary, by temperament as much as by necessity, I relished doing this when weaker hearts did not.[9]

Thatcher was not interested in overthrowing traditional British institutions. While she would certainly have been a Republican had she been born an American, in Britain she was not a *republican*. She supported the traditional pillars of British society—the Monarchy, Parliament, and the Church of England. She led a revolt against the socialism and collectivism that were destroying traditional British life and against Communists in the Soviet Union who were trying to spread collectivism around the world.

The Crown represents more than a thousand years of continuity in British history, Parliament the ancient liberties of the British people, and the Church of England the Christian faith that shaped British civilization.

When you add to these the ancient universities of Oxford and Cambridge, the top "public schools" (i.e., private boarding schools) such as Eton and Harrow, the civil service, and the press, you have the traditional British Establishment—inherently conservative in its traditions and prerogatives but not necessarily members of the Conservative Party. Thatcher supported these institutions as prime minister (though they did not always support her), but her conservatism reflected different values, which is why it is called Thatcherism.

Thatcherism is in the best sense "conservative" because it conserves or seeks to restore the best traditions of Britain. Thatcher told her Asian audiences that she did not invent Thatcherism: "I and my colleagues rediscovered it. The values, ideas and beliefs which I was privileged to be able to put into effect in Britain in the eleven and a half years of my Prime Ministership were rooted in the experience of the past and reinforced by events in my lifetime." She added, "But my outlook was also shaped by my country itself and its history—above all its political history. How could it not be? For I was always fascinated by politics. For me the name of Britain was synonymous with freedom, justice and democracy."[10]

Family and Community Values

Throughout her career, Margaret Thatcher observed that Thatcherism is a restatement of older principles and values applied to a modern setting, and that events in her life led to its formulation. There was, for instance, always the influence of her family on what would become Thatcherism decades later. "My ideals, like those of most people, were first shaped by my family—a Christian family believing in the sanctity of the individual and that each of us is responsible and accountable for his own actions."[11] Without the influence of her family, there never would have been Thatcherism. As she moved into 10 Downing Street in 1979, she commented, "I just owe almost everything to my own father. I really do. He brought me up to believe all the things that I do believe and they're just the values on which I've fought the Election. And it's passionately interesting for me that the things that I learned in a small town, in a very modest home, are just the things that I believe have won the Election."[12]

Long before she read about "the theoretical advantages of monetarism, free trade and deregulation,"[13] Thatcher learned about the economy and society from her family.[14] As she once put it in a television interview, "I think the most important thing of them all, the greatest gift of all, is having a family. Home is two things: it is both a refuge and it is an inspiration and it goes across the generations. You have always got home to go to, and I think that the people who have not really miss the greatest thing in life, and I think it is extremely important to keep that going."[15]

At the corner of North Parade and Broad Street, in Grantham, Lincolnshire, there was a grocer's shop and post office with an apartment above them. The building is still there, bearing a small plaque recognizing its historical significance: "Birthplace of the Rt. Hon. Margaret Thatcher, MP, first woman Prime Minister of Great Britain and Northern Ireland." To this day, it is the only memorial to Margaret Thatcher in Grantham. Her father, Alfred Roberts, was the proprietor of a specialist grocery. The family lived "over the shop," as Thatcher put it. "Wonderful aromas of spices, coffee and smoked hams would waft through the house," she recalled.[16] She learned "that it was international trade which brought tea, coffee, sugar and spices to those who frequented our shop."[17] Thatcher was a free trader from the beginning.

The Roberts house stands some one hundred yards from the Grantham railway tracks. The town is located on the London-to-Edinburgh East Coast Main Line, a major passenger rail artery connecting Britain's capital city with northern England and Scotland. "We could set our clocks by the 'Flying Scotsman' as it thundered through," Thatcher wrote[18] of the train that has been running between London and Edinburgh since 1862.

Grantham is south of Lincoln and east of Nottingham in the East Midlands—the British equivalent of Middle America. The area's ties with America go back to the first Puritan settlement in the Massachusetts Bay Colony, which was named after the Lincolnshire town of Boston, due east of Grantham. "We were immensely proud of our town," Thatcher remembered, "we knew its history and traditions; we were glad to be part of its life."[19]

Margaret Thatcher may be the most famous person from Grantham in modern times, but its most illustrious student was the physicist and mathematician Sir Isaac Newton (1642–1727), who was born nearby and attended the King's School in Grantham. Margaret Roberts attended another grammar school (a selective state school) in town, Kesteven and Grantham Girls' School, finishing first in her class in 1943. After Grantham, Newton went to Cambridge, but Miss Roberts chose Oxford, where she entered Somerville College. The only British prime minister to hold a degree in science (chemistry), she studied under Dorothy Hodgkin, a pioneer in X-ray crystallography who later won the Nobel Prize. Margaret Thatcher's later career in politics did not win her friends in the overwhelmingly left-wing faculty at Oxford, and the university denied her the honorary degree that would be expected for the first woman prime minister. Her papers are now archived alongside Winston Churchill's at Churchill College, Cambridge.[20]

Life "over the shop" is an important part of Thatcherism, whose namesake lived "over the shop" twice in her life: as a girl and as prime minister. At 10 Downing Street, the official residence of the British prime minister, Thatcher and her husband, Denis, occupied a small apartment at the top of the historic residence for eleven and a half years. "Every practical consideration suggested it, as well as my own taste for long hours of work," she remembers. "As we used to say, harking back to my girlhood in Grantham, I liked living over the shop."[21]

It may seem strange to Americans that the head of the British government lives in a small apartment. Of course, there is also Chequers, the stately country residence of the prime minister in Buckinghamshire, similar to the U.S. president's Camp David. But the symbolism of prime ministers' living and working in a London townhouse, however upscale, is important. The positions of head of state and head of government, which are united in the American presidency, are divided in the United Kingdom. The Queen is the head of state, and she therefore lives in a palace. Less grand accommodation is provided to her first ministers. In fact, not every prime minister has lived at 10 Downing Street. Some had better houses and preferred private over public housing, while others were uncomfortable with the complement of staff, meeting rooms, and offices—it is an office building as much as a house—and just never settled in. When Labour's Ramsay MacDonald was in office, he could be seen knocking on the front door to be let in.

Thatcher spent seven years more over the shop at One North Parade in Grantham than she did at 10 Downing Street. "Life 'over the shop' is much more than a phrase," she recorded, "It is something which those who have lived it know to be quite distinctive."[22] She "lived" her family's business and had to do her share of the work in addition to studying hard at school. The family worked long hours to make a living, and Margaret learned the necessities and virtues of hard work and thrift.

She also sampled her first taste of civic life in Grantham. Alfred Roberts was a local councilor, alderman, and mayor at one time or another, and people talked about local issues in his shop. He was also active in the Methodist Church and in civic organizations, including Rotary. His daughter was a natural politician on the hustings, relying on training that began in the corner shop, where the Roberts family had always been on call, day and night. In Grantham, she developed a lifelong passion for discussion and debate.

In a telling passage from her memoirs, Thatcher contrasted her own local economic training in Grantham to the formative influences on John Maynard Keynes and the upper-class, left-wing Bloomsbury Group—an odd collection of fashionable artists, writers, poets, and philosophers who inhabited the Bloomsbury section of central London in the first few decades of the twentieth century. She observed that "extant economists are no less the slaves of outside influences. That was true of Keynes himself— a member of the 'Bloomsbury' set whose rejection of the Victorian virtues in their own behaviour was subtly but surely echoed in the abandonment of the classical liberal rules and restraints in economics with which 'Keynes-ianism' became synonymous."[23] She continued, "So too my own views on economics flowed from personal experience of the world in which I grew up. My 'Bloomsbury' was Grantham—Methodism, the grocer's shop, Rotary and all the serious, sober virtues cultivated and esteemed in that environment."[24] Thatcher concluded, "There is no better course for under-standing free-market economics than life in a corner shop."[25]

She made the same point in Seoul in 1992: The "desire to do better for one's family is the great dynamo of progress. Most people work, save, invest, invent, adapt and trade for this one reason, which goes to the root of their very being."[26] One of the great lessons from Grantham was that "the fruits of liberty are so rich and varied, because liberty is creative. And that in turn is why wealth is not generated by Government; it is as Adam Smith observed the enterprise of individual men and women which cre-ates the 'Wealth of Nations.'"[27] She noted in her autobiography that "the kind of life that the people of Grantham had lived before the [Second World War] *was* a decent and wholesome one, and its values were shaped by the community rather than by the government."[28]

Thatcher and Victorian Virtues

Margaret Thatcher was often accused by her political opponents and the liberal media of trying to reestablish "Victorian values" (or Victorian virtues, as she preferred to call them)[29] long after they were thought to have been consigned to history. In fact, Thatcherism was considered synonymous with Victorian values, and she was frequently asked why she believed they were important. The reason was simple. Victorian values, she said in 1983, "were the values when our country became great, but not only did our country become great internationally, also so much advance was made in this country."[30] In Thatcher's view, Victorian virtues were "fundamental."[31]

In the permissive era that began in the 1960s, "Victorian" was a purely pejorative adjective, especially when applied to morality. It meant old-fashioned and oppressive. Yet in an interview with the *Financial Times* in 1987, Thatcher issued a vigorous and unapologetic call for the restoration of Victorian virtues.[32]

As she often pointed out, the Victorian era was one of tremendous progress for Britain. By the time of Queen Victoria's Diamond Jubilee in 1897, Britain was the world's greatest power, with a standard of living that was envied across much of the world. For the first time in history, the majority of the British population enjoyed meaningful economic and social progress. The miseries of two World Wars and the Great Depression lay ahead, but for most British families, the last years of Victoria's reign and the Edwardian period that followed were the best they would see until the second half of the twentieth century.

In the nineteenth century, the British economy realized the full benefits of the Industrial Revolution. The country became the "workshop of the world," producing goods on a scale unimaginable a generation or two earlier. The Victorian era also saw the rise of the British Empire as a great force for good on the world stage. "The fact remains," insists the historian

Niall Ferguson, "that no organization in history has done more to promote the free movement of goods, capital and labour than the British Empire in the nineteenth and twentieth centuries. And no organization has done more to impose Western norms of law, order and governance around the world…. Without the spread of British rule around the world, it is hard to believe that the structures of liberal capitalism would have been so successfully established in so many different economies around the world."[33]

Liberalism Used to Mean Freedom

In the Victorian age, "liberalism" meant freedom, not big government as it does today. Margaret Thatcher described her father as an "old-fashioned liberal," noting that "[i]ndividual responsibility was his watchword and sound finance his passion. He was an admirer of John Stuart Mill's *On Liberty*."[34] This kind of liberalism is part of the British character, as Thatcher often attested. Her own political philosophy, she said, "would be best described as 'liberal,' in the old-fashioned sense. And I mean the liberalism of Mr. Gladstone [the great Victorian leader of the Liberal Party] not of the latter day collectivists."[35]

The Victorians abhorred wasteful spending, believed in free trade, and actually shrank the size of their government. Milton and Rose Friedman pointed out that "government spending fell as a fraction of national income—from close to one-quarter of the national income early in the nineteenth century to about one-tenth of national income at the time of Queen Victoria's Jubilee in 1897, when Britain was at the very apex of its power and glory."[36]

The Victorians also presided over a relatively peaceful century as far as Britain was concerned. From the defeat of Napoleon at Waterloo in 1815 until the outbreak of World War I in the summer of 1914, British domination of the seas guaranteed free trade, and a balance of power in

Europe maintained the peace. To be sure, there were several wars across the British Empire (including the Anglo-Boer Wars) and unrest in Ireland, but none of them threatened Britain itself. The conflicts were limited in scope and mainly outside of Europe, with the notable exception of the Crimean War of 1853–1856.

Political freedom grew with economic freedom, and the voting franchise was dramatically extended over the course of the nineteenth century. There was also more religious freedom than ever before, which led to greater piety. Nonconformists, including the Roberts family's Methodists, were able to practice their faith freely outside the established church. Even the lives of Roman Catholics improved dramatically, as most sanctions were lifted and a string of prominent converts brought a measure of respectability to a once despised minority. The result of this freedom was one of the greatest religious awakenings in Christian history, which led, under the leadership of William Wilberforce, to the abolition of slavery in the British Empire.

Victorian values were based on Christianity, and the Bible was the official guide. Thatcher herself described the importance of the Bible in British life:

> As we emerged from the twilight of medieval times, when for many life was characterised by tyranny, injustice and cruelty, so we became what one historian has described as "the people of a book and that book was the Bible". (J. R. Green). What he meant, I think, was that this nation adopted albeit gradually— a system of government and a way of living together which reflected the values implicit in that Book. We acknowledged as a nation that God was the source of our strength and that the teachings of Christ applied to our national as well as our personal life.[37]

Despite the extraordinary achievements of the Victorian era, the Left wants to talk only about its problems, many of which were resolved through Christian values and charity. Socialists unfairly depict the period as one of ruthless capitalism, brutal imperialism, inequality, shocking working conditions in factories for men, women, and children, and urban squalor—all part of their coordinated attack on capitalism and freedom.

"The Victorian age has been very badly treated in socialist propaganda," Thatcher reminded an audience of young Conservatives.[38] She later said that she "wish[ed] that those who criticise our Victorian predecessors for their undoubted failures were able or willing to emulate some of their achievements."[39]

Thatcherism and Christian Faith

In Margaret Thatcher's childhood, she recalled, "[o]ur lives revolved around Methodism":[40] church services twice on Sundays, Sunday school, prayer services during the week, practicing hymns on the piano. The Roberts household kept the Sabbath in a way any Victorian would have recognized. Thatcher remembered listening to exceptional sermons in provincial Grantham: "The sermons we heard every Sunday made a great impact on me."[41] She told the journalist David Frost that "religion is a fundamentally important factor in the life of everyone in this country.... The ideals of democracy are founded upon human rights, and the dignity of the individual is something that comes not from statecraft, but something which really comes on Biblical foundations."[42]

It is easy to forget that excellent preaching was important in the development of Protestant churches in Britain and America, and the lines between the laity and clergy were often blurred. In addition to his work in business and civic life, Alfred Roberts was a Methodist lay preacher. He left school when he was thirteen, as was the practice for working families at the time, and was largely self-taught. Lay preachers' lack of theological education was more than offset by natural devotion and understanding of Scripture unmatched then or now. In fact, one of the greatest preachers in nineteenth-century Anglican England, C. H. Spurgeon, was actually a Baptist who had neither formal theological training nor a university degree (his father and grandfather had also been preachers). He began his career teaching Sunday school at St. Andrew's Street Baptist Church in Cambridge and was a pastor in London by the age of twenty.

Based at the Finkin Street Methodist Church, Roberts was a popular preacher in Grantham. "He was a powerful preacher whose sermons contained a good deal of intellectual substance," his daughter remembered.[43] She also recalled his "sermon voice," and she once asked him why he used it. Roberts was "taken aback" by this question, but Thatcher always considered it an "unconscious homage to the biblical message."[44] After hearing her address his congregation in Finchley in 1971, the minister Leonard Barnett said that Thatcher herself would have made "a splendid Methodist preacher."[45]

Even among Thatcher's most ardent admirers in America, few know much about her personal beliefs. Two addresses that she delivered at the Anglican church of St. Lawrence Jewry are therefore of special interest. Located in the yard of the Guildhall in what was the medieval Jewish ghetto, St. Lawrence Jewry is the official church of the Lord Mayor and the City of London Corporation. She spoke there first on March 30, 1978, while still leader of the Opposition in Parliament. Sounding more like a Victorian Evangelical than a late twentieth-century politician, Thatcher spoke of her religious upbringing and how life on this earth was preparation for eternal life. "I was brought up, let me remind you, in a religious environment which, by the standards of today, would seem very rigid," she said. "What mattered fundamentally was Man's relationship to God, and in the last resort this depended on the response of the individual soul to God's Grace."[46] The old Victorian concern with Judgment Day should guide any political philosophy, she observed. Politics was "about establishing the conditions in which men and women can best use their fleeting lives in this world to prepare themselves for the next."[47] She concluded, "I was also brought up to believe that it was only through whole-hearted devotion to this preparation that true earthly happiness could be achieved. Experience gives me no reason to revise this view."[48]

Thatcher returned to St. Lawrence Jewry three years later, in March 1981, this time as prime minister.[49] Interrupted by hecklers from the Young Communist League, she nevertheless delivered a powerful address straight from the heart. She stressed the great importance of Christian values in society, reminding her audience that "the virtue of a nation is only as great as the virtue of the individuals who compose it." She emphasized the importance of "personal moral responsibility," a core element of Thatcherism: "We must always beware of supposing that somehow we can get rid of our own moral duties by handing them over to the community; that somehow we can get rid of our own guilt by talking about 'national' or 'social' guilt. We are called on to repent our own sins, not each other's sins."

In the second St. Lawrence Jewry speech, Thatcher praised the vision of two great Victorian philanthropists who had fought against the evils of slavery and inhumane working conditions. William Wilberforce and Lord Shaftesbury were, in Thatcher's words, leaders "motivated first and foremost by their Christian beliefs." She pointed out that "it is also significant that most of the great philanthropists who set up schools and hospitals did so because they saw this as part of their Christian service for the people of the nation." She held up the Victorian era, with its Christian ethos and emphasis on private philanthropy, to argue that the role of government must be strictly limited and based on Christian values:

> As for the role of the state (what the Bible calls the things that are Caesar's), I have never concealed my own philosophy. I

believe it is a philosophy which rests on Christian assumptions, though I fully recognise that some Christians would have a different view. To me the wisdom of statesmanship consists of— knowing the limits within which government can and ought to act for the good of the individuals who make up society;— respecting those limits;—ensuring that the laws to which the people are subject shall be just, and consistent with the public conscience;—making certain that those laws are firmly and fairly enforced;—making the nation strong for the defence of its way of life against potential aggression;—and maintaining an honest currency. Only Governments can carry out these functions, and in these spheres Government must be strong.

Thatcher called for "a national purpose," one that "must include the defence of the values which we believe to be of vital importance." She made an emphatic plea for the renewal of "the spirit of the nation," and made it clear that "I believe the spirit of this nation is a Christian one. The values which sustain our way of life have by no means disappeared but they are in danger of being undermined."

She reiterated these themes in a major address to the General Assembly of the Church of Scotland in May 1988, during her third and last term as prime minister, calling for the defense of the Judaic-Christian tradition in Britain. "[T]he Christian religion," Thatcher noted, "which, of course, embodies many of the great spiritual and moral truths of Judaism—is a fundamental part of our national heritage. And I believe it is the wish of the overwhelming majority of people that this heritage should be preserved and fostered. For centuries it has been our very life blood. And indeed we are a nation whose ideals are founded on the Bible."[50]

These speeches show that Thatcher's deeply held religious values were a major influence on her political thinking. Her Christianity placed her at odds with the big-government tenets of socialism, which were ravaging Britain in the 1970s.

Rolling Back Socialism

In a speech at Hofstra University in 2000, Margaret Thatcher remarked that it was no coincidence that the Soviet Union had flexed its muscles all over the world in the 1970s, when socialism was at its apex in Britain:

> If today that statement seems alarmist, please remember that this was also the high point of Soviet expansionism, and that the same socialist politicians who were keenest to impose a left-wing blue-print on Britain were often deeply sympathetic to the advance of Soviet power abroad. What occurred in Britain in this period was not therefore just a clash between two parties, it was a struggle between two systems offering two entirely different destinies.[51]

Peaceful coexistence between the Soviet Union and the West had become a path toward collectivism everywhere. Whether it was collectivism in Britain or the Soviet Union, the Iron Lady viewed it as a threat to freedom. She first read Friedrich Hayek's *The Road to Serfdom* while a student at Oxford. The book made a lasting impression on her, particularly its dedication, "To Socialists of All Parties." Hayek maintained that there was ultimately no difference in the objectives of socialism, communism, and fascism: "The various kinds of collectivism, communism, fascism, etc., differ among themselves in the nature of the goal toward which they want to direct the efforts of society. But they all differ from liberalism and individualism in wanting to organize the whole of society...."[52] He added that socialism was not only the most important variety of collectivism, but it had "persuaded liberal-minded people to submit once more to that regimentation of economic life which they had over-thrown...."[53] As Thatcher relates in her memoirs, her father did not leave the Liberal Party; the Liberal Party left him. "Like many other business people he had, as it were, been left behind by the Liberal Party's acceptance of collectivism."[54] Reflecting the influence of Hayek, Thatcher declared, "The proponents of these [collectivist] ideologies engaged in polemics and indeed violence against each other. But they had more in common than they admitted. For their essence was that the state had the right, indeed the duty, to act like God. And the results were devilish."[55]

Thatcher admitted that she had not "fully grasped the implications of Hayek's little masterpiece" as a student. It was only in the 1970s when Britain was in economic and financial turmoil brought on by socialism that *The Road to Serfdom* climbed to "the top of [her] reading list."[56] And it was not only Hayek's withering criticism of collectivism that attracted her—his "unanswerable criticisms of socialism"[57]—but also his view that the best government operated along the lines of classical liberalism: "The kind of state Conservatives find congenial"—in her words—"a limited government under a rule of law."[58] As Walter Bagehot wrote of the English in 1867, "We look on State action, not as our own action, but as alien action; as an imposed tyranny from without, not as the consummated result of our own organised wishes."[59] The rediscovery of this tradition was one of the great contributions that Thatcher bequeathed to Britain and the world. As she wrote in *The Downing Street Years*, during her time as prime minister, Britain "was the first country to reverse the onward march of socialism."[60] This reversal of socialism in Britain "re-established our reputation as a nation of innovators and entrepreneurs."[61]

While socialist thought in Britain goes back to the nineteenth century, with a good deal of famous names associated with its development, it was not until after 1945 that socialism was actually implemented there. World War II led to unprecedented government control of key aspects of the

British economy. The objective was clear: winning the war at all costs. Survival after 1939 required tremendous sacrifice by all. This included a coalition government of Conservatives, Liberals, and Labour from 1940, with Winston Churchill in charge. While Churchill was always an opponent of socialism, he had to focus on winning the war, and delegated domestic policy, particularly postwar planning, to the left-of-center members of the coalition government. As Thatcher remembers, "The Second World War, even more than other wars, had given an enormous boost to government control. Indeed, oddly enough when you consider that it was fought against totalitarian states, the War provided in many people's minds convincing proof that a planned society and a planned economy worked best."[62]

The famous Beveridge Report of 1942 laid the foundation for the modern British welfare state. Officially styled the *Report of the Inter-Departmental Committee on Social Insurance and Allied Services*, it was written by Sir William Beveridge, a social reformer and the director of the then left-leaning London School of Economics. Beveridge's goals were the "abolition of want" and "cradle to the grave" security. To achieve them, Beveridge proposed a National Health Service, social insurance, family assistance, and full employment. When combined with the economic theories of John Maynard Keynes, who believed that government could manage the economy through fiscal policy, the stage was set for an unprecedented expansion of the state.

The reforms proposed by the coalition government were popular with the British people, who remembered the poverty and unemployment of the 1930s and looked forward to a new start after the war. For many in the government, expansion of the welfare state was the reward that the British people deserved for their wartime sacrifices. The Labour Party benefited from the popularity of social reforms and the promise of a better life. While Churchill remained a hero with the British people, his

Conservative Party was associated with the unemployment, poverty, and appeasement of the 1930s. In the July 1945 election, conducted two months after victory in Europe, British voters turned to the Labour Party to rebuild their war-torn economy.

When Thatcher was asked about the Beveridge Report after she became leader of the Conservative Party, she did not voice objections. Postwar planning occurred, she said, because the British "had faith in the future, in our ability to rise again." She found the fault not with postwar planning itself but with socialists who had drawn the wrong conclusions about the welfare state. "Churchill's concept of the Welfare State was that society needed a ladder and a safety net," Thatcher argued, "a ladder by which people could improve their lot by effort, and a safety net below which nobody could fall. Post-war Labour Governments produced the safety net, but cut down the ladder."[63] Yet she always drew a distinction between the welfare state and compassion, because many on the Left equated the two:

> The state cannot generate compassion; it can and must provide a "safety net" for those who, through no fault of their own, are unable to cope on their own. There is need for far more generosity in our national life, but generosity is born in the hearts of men and women; it cannot be manufactured by politicians, and assuredly it will not flourish if politicians foster the illusion that the exercise of compassion can be left to officials.[64]

A major problem of the welfare state, as Hayek noted, was that it produced inflation.[65] The temptation to debase the currency to reduce the financial obligation of providing all the benefits associated with the welfare state bedeviled both British and American fiscal and monetary policies after 1945. In Thatcher's view, inflation was not only an economic but a moral problem. As she said in 1981:

> In terms of ethics and national economics, I should like also to refer to what I believe is an evil, namely sustained inflation. For over thirty years the value of our currency has been eroding. It is an insidious evil because its effects are slow to be seen and relatively painless in the short run. Yet it has a morally debilitating influence on all aspects of our national life. It reduces the value of savings and therefore thrift, it undermines financial agreements, it stimulates hostility between workers and employers over matters of pay, it encourages debt and it diminishes the prospects of jobs.[66]

The Labour government under Clement Attlee viewed the welfare state as only part of a larger socialist plan for Britain. It was also committed to the traditional socialist goal of nationalizing the means of production, distribution, and exchange. With its large majority from 1945 to 1951, the Labour government nationalized mines, railways, civilian aviation, road transport, gas and electric utilities, as well as the Bank of England, and created the National Health Service. This resulted in a huge addition to the government payroll, with a large chunk of the workforce employed by the nationalized industries. The National Health Service remains to this day one of the largest employers in the world.[67]

The period from 1945 to 1979 was the great era of government central planning and collectivism, and the Conservative Party largely acquiesced. Some Conservatives wanted to appear modern. Others, fearing electoral defeat, adopted a position of being better managers of collectivism. Successive Conservative governments from 1951 to 1974, with few exceptions, refused or failed to overturn Labour's postwar socialist program. A "consensus" emerged across party lines on a broad range of policies that preserved the status quo. There were attempts to break out of the consensus. But when any opposition appeared, and in the 1970s the opposition turned violent, the Tories always raised the white flag.

Consensus politics was a leading cause of Britain's postwar economic decline. Both parties continued to subsidize large nationalized industries, increase spending on the welfare state, and follow Keynesian economic policies. For a while, all appeared to go well. Britain enjoyed a period of relative prosperity in the 1950s with recovery of the global economy after the war, a shift by the nationalized industries to peacetime production, and the continued lifting of wartime rationing and controls by the Conservative government under Churchill after 1951. It seemed to many that Keynesian full-employment policies combined with nationalized industries were working.

Thatcher remembered the 1950s in particular as a relatively happy time because life finally returned to normal after the war. Rationing ended in the mid-1950s, and new and old consumer goods returned to the store shelves. In 1957, the Conservative prime minister Harold Macmillan boasted that "most of our people have never had it so good."[68] The Tories won three electoral victories in a row between 1951 and 1959, the last of which brought the young Margaret Thatcher to Parliament.

Macmillan was right that the British people had never had it so good, but he worried that it was too good to last: "For, amidst all this prosperity, there is one problem that has troubled us—in one way or another—ever since the war. It's the problem of rising prices. Our constant concern today is—can prices be steadied while at the same time we maintain full employment in an expanding economy? Can we control inflation? This is the problem of our time."[69]

The answer was no—the British government could not control inflation any more than it could control the British weather. And Macmillan
was one of the reasons why. Inflation was symptomatic of larger problems
with socialism, since the government set wages and prices and employment for the large segments of the economy that had been nationalized.
"… Macmillan's leadership edged the [Conservative] Party in the direction
of state intervention," Thatcher noted, "a trend which would become
much more marked after 1959."[70] In 1961, in a vain attempt to gain better
control of the British economy, Macmillan established the National Economic Development Council, or "Neddy," a tripartite council composed
of representatives from government, management, and unions to recommend pro-growth economic policies. Neddy was an important step along
the road of economic planning for the whole economy. Macmillan also
established the National Incomes Commission, or "Nicky," to control
incomes but faced labor union opposition, foreshadowing trouble in the
future. As Thatcher remembered, "It was, after all, none other than Harold
Macmillan who in 1938 proposed in his influential book *The Middle Way*
to extend state control and planning over a wide range of production and
services."[71] Macmillan, whose family had published Keynes's work, was
himself a Keynesian. In these ways, he represented the postwar consensus.

The Conservatives were defeated in 1964 and again in 1966 by Harold
Wilson and the Labour Party. The elections showed that whenever there
is a choice between conservatives acting like socialists and the real thing,
voters usually go for the real thing. By the 1960s it was clear that the key
to Conservative victory was not in propping up socialism, Thatcher wrote,
but in an "ideological clash of opposing political parties as essential to the
effective functioning of democracy. The pursuit of 'consensus,' therefore,
was fundamentally subversive of popular choice."[72] It was a theme she
returned to often. Less than a month before the 1979 election, she declared

to an audience in Wales, "The Old Testament prophets didn't go out into the highways saying, 'Brothers, I want consensus.' They said, 'This is my faith and my vision! This is what I passionately believe!' And they preached it. We have a message. Go out, preach it, practice it, fight for it—and the day will be ours!"[73]

The 1970s saw the postwar consensus finally collapse. The decade was "the high point (if that's the word) of socialism," Thatcher noted in her Hofstra speech, a decade after she left office.[74] "Britain was on a knife edge," and Conservatives had to "reverse the ratchet," she added. "The notion of the ratchet," she said, "… reflected the fact that Britain's post-War history had consisted of sharp swings to the left, followed by periods when the leftward lurch was arrested but never reversed. The result was that an ever greater share of a virtually stagnant economy was under the control of the state."[75] She reminded her American audience of how serious the situation in Britain was in 1970s: "One more jerk of the ratchet and we would create a probably irreversible shift towards state power and away from liberty."[76]

Liberty

Margaret Thatcher had one solution to collectivist ideologies: liberty. Collectivism in all its forms is antithetical to the British and American political tradition of freedom. "Liberty—or freedom if you like—is a perfectly simple concept, understandable to all, it seems, except to the very dim or the very clever."[77] She defined it for her audience as "the condition in which a man (or woman) is free to express their identity, exercise their God-given talents, acquire and pass on property, bring up a family, succeed or fail, live and die in peace. And the most important requirement for that free society is a rule of law, informed by equity and upheld by impartial judges."[78]

The best way to secure liberty is through government policies that are anchored in human nature. "Given the right framework of laws, taxes and regulation, most individuals will apply their talents and energies productively," Thatcher said. And the key to such policies is always clear: limited government. She concluded that individuals "will certainly make far more effort on behalf of themselves and their families than they ever would for an impersonal entity called 'government.'"[79]

Liberty was never an abstract concept to Thatcher. It was grounded in the history and character of the British people. Freedom and British history, she believed, were inseparable. "You sometimes hear people say, 'what have I got to conserve?'" she said in 1983. "Instinctively we know that the answer is 'a vast amount'. A tolerant and fairminded country. Personal liberty, protected by the rule of law. Democratic institutions defended by armed forces who serve rather than rule."[80]

The Conservative Party, in one form or another, has "conserved" the Crown, the Church, and Parliament and upheld the British Constitution. The colonists in America may have rebelled against the British government in 1776, but they did not rebel against the liberties that were their birthright as British subjects. Instead they demanded that these liberties be returned to them. Before the Stamp Act, Benjamin Franklin maintained, Americans "considered the Parliament as the great bulwark and security of their liberties."[81]

In 1989 the French celebrated the two hundredth anniversary of their revolution. With the motto of *Liberté, Égalité, Fraternité*, the modern age of equality and human rights was supposedly launched—at least in the minds of "progressive historians." It was more a dress rehearsal of the horrors that the world would face after the Russian Revolution. Proud of their blood-soaked revolution, the French held a grand ceremony in Paris, which coincided with a G7 summit meeting. For the thoughtful Thatcher, however, it was an occasion not to celebrate a revolution but to reflect on how traditional British liberty differed from the variety that led to the guillotine.

"For me as a British Conservative," Thatcher wrote in her memoirs, "with Edmund Burke the father of Conservatism and first perceptive critic of the Revolution as my ideological mentor, the events of 1789 represent a perennial illusion in politics."[82] Rather than launching liberty as British and Americans understand the term, the French launched "purges, mass murder, and war," all "in the name of abstract ideas, formulated by vain intellectuals."[83] She noted with evident disdain that the bicentennial festivities included an opera, "with pride of place in the set being given to a huge guillotine."[84]

The French Revolution is an emblem of one of the great misunderstandings of the modern age:

> The single biggest intellectual error during my political lifetime has been to confuse freedom with equality. In fact, equality—being an unnatural condition which can only be enforced by the state—is usually the enemy of liberty. This was a point I made in France on the bicentennial celebration of the French Revolution, which deliberately and dangerously confused the two. My French hosts were somewhat perplexed. But the point stands.[85]

She contrasted British freedom with the *liberté* of the French Revolution, whose leaders thought they could decree liberty with the stroke of a pen. "The English tradition of liberty, however, grew over the centuries: its most marked features are continuity, respect for law and a sense of balance, as demonstrated by the Glorious Revolution of 1688."[86] Traditionally it has been argued that the Glorious Revolution was one of the key events in preserving ancient British liberties, when Parliament asserted its control over the Crown and a Bill of Rights was enacted in 1689. Thereafter, the sovereignty of Parliament was firmly established and its role as guarantor of British freedoms affirmed. Walter Bagehot expressed the genius of the British Constitution: "our freedom is the result of centuries of resistance, more or less legal, or more or less illegal, more or less audacious, or more or less timid, to the executive government." He concluded, "The natural impulse of the English people is to resist authority."[87] This resistance to authority erupted in 1688 and 1776, and it reappeared in 1975, when the Conservative Party chose Margaret Thatcher to be its leader.

As Thatcher told a French interviewer in 1989, liberty and human rights did not begin with the French Revolution. The idea of liberty predated the French Revolution by centuries and has its origins in the Judaic-Christian tradition and Anglo-American history. The French Revolution added nothing to this history. "I was asked [in Paris] about human rights and whether I thought human rights started two hundred years ago," Thatcher said. "Most certainly they did not and I gave the reasons why they go right back to Judaism, to Christianity, they go right back to Magna Carta, they go right back to our Bill of Rights, 1689 after we had our 1688. The American Statement of Independence 1776 was one of the most brilliant pieces of English literature in proclaiming the liberties of man and the government is there to serve the liberties of man."[88]

Thatcherism will endure. The British historian Andrew Roberts has observed, "Seldom does the emergence of a single individual undeniably change the course of history.... The principles that she established—which together form the coherent political program called Thatcherism—have perhaps more relevance now than at any time since the 1980s. To write her off as a historical figure is to discard the timelessness, and thus the most important aspect, of her political thought."[89]

Key Leadership Lessons

- Thatcher showed how faith and family are critically important drivers of successful leadership. She demonstrated how effective leadership values can be forged by strong families and churches.

- Do not be afraid to talk about the role of Christian virtues in advancing a free and prosperous society, including self-reliance, thrift, and helping others without depending on the intervention of the state.

- Defend the traditional values that have been the backbone of the West's success for the last two hundred years, even though the Left may deride them as outdated or unfashionable.

- Great leaders are willing to reject consensus politics and forge their own path. Thatcherism was based on a determination to stand up to the status quo and Establishment.

- Americans should be proud of their history, as Thatcher was of British history, and conservatives should not let liberals denigrate its greatness or rewrite it to further their agenda.

- Government does not have a monopoly on compassion. Free people cannot shift moral responsibility to politicians and bureaucrats. The cornerstone of all freedom is individual liberty and the rule of law, not government power and control.

CHAPTER THREE

THE TWILIGHT OF SOCIALIST BRITAIN

"Some Socialists seem to believe that people should be numbers in a State computer. We believe they should be individuals."
—MARGARET THATCHER, SPEECH TO CONSERVATIVE PARTY CONFERENCE, OCTOBER 10, 1975[1]

The 1970s: Economic Freedom under Siege

Four decades on, it is easy to forget how dreadful the economic situation was in Britain in the 1970s. The country was plagued by the so-called "British disease": a destructive combination of high taxes, high inflation, high unemployment, chronic strikes, crippling deficits and debt, low worker productivity, unprofitable nation-alized industries, and international weakness. The "British disease" was the legacy of three decades of socialism and Keynesian economic policy. The history of Britain in the 1970s is also a lesson for Americans, as the Obama administration is leading the United States in a direction eerily similar to that of Britain.

Any selection of economic statistics from the 1970s shows that Britain, the birthplace of the Industrial Revolution, was in serious trouble. From 1968 to 1973, average annual output grew by 3.2 percent, but employment rose only by 0.2 percent, and inflation increased by 7.9 percent. The "Swinging Sixties" were over, and the trouble that Harold Macmillan had warned about a decade earlier had arrived. From 1973 to 1979, only the most ardent socialists maintained any confidence in the future. The average annual growth in output fell to 1.4 percent, and employment growth remained constant at 0.2 percent (with unemployment rising), while inflation doubled to 16 percent.[2]

The troubling signs of economic decline were also evident in the figures for output per worker, which plunged from 1973 to 1979.[3] From 1970 to 1980, Britain trailed all its economic partners in this measure, including the United States, Canada, France, West Germany, and Italy.[4] Declining output per worker also signaled declining productivity. British labor productivity began to drop after 1973[5] and soon lagged far behind France and West Germany.[6]

Rising unemployment and inflation added to the misery. From 1948 to 1970, the British unemployment rate never reached 3 percent, but from 1970 to 1979, it was below 3 percent for only three years.[7] Unemployment during the decade rose as high as five times postwar lows.[8] The postwar commitment to full employment, a central feature of Keynesianism and the welfare state, was falling apart. Yet while unemployment was rising fast, inflation was rising even faster, confounding many economists. From 1972 to 1977, when inflation was a problem for most of the countries in the Organization for Economic Cooperation and Development, British inflation was twice as bad as the OECD average.[9] According to the Bank of England, "Inflation in the UK got out of control in the 1970s. It averaged 13 percent a year, and peaked at 25 percent in 1975."[10] Britain was on the precipice of hyperinflation, a rarity in developed countries. After 1973, the annual inflation rate remained well above 10 percent except in 1978.[11]

British decline was spelled out dramatically in a famous dispatch of March 31, 1979, from Sir Nicholas Henderson, the retiring ambassador to France (whom Thatcher would soon post to the United States). Britain had fallen so far behind its European competitors, particularly Germany and France, in labor productivity and GDP growth, he wrote, that the once great country was now "poor and unproud."[12] Henderson lamented, "It is our decline since [the mid-1950s] in relation to our European partners that has been so marked, so that today we are not only no longer a world power, but we are not in the first rank even as a European one. Income per head in Britain is now, for the first time for over 300 years, below that in France."[13] Henderson's dispatch remains one the best analyses from inside the government of how low Britain had fallen on the eve of Margaret Thatcher's election as prime minister.

The Rise of Keynesianism

The United States had economic problems in the 1970s similar to Britain's, but they were less severe mainly because America had not followed the socialist path that Britain did after World War II. The Republicans, who won control of the House and Senate in 1946, were able to dismantle many wartime controls on the economy—the sort of controls that gave socialism its footing in Britain.[14]

The socialist threat to America had been real enough. The political analyst Michael Barone reminds us, "Franklin Roosevelt in his January 1944 State of the Union address echoed the Beveridge Report."[15] The president called for "steeply graduated taxes, government controls on crop prices and food prices [and] continued controls on wages.... Government should guarantee everyone a job, an education, and clothing, housing, medical care, and financial security against the risks of old age and sickness."[16] It was Roosevelt's view that "[t]rue individual freedom cannot exist without economic security and independence."[17]

If Roosevelt's death in April 1945 and the Republican takeover of Congress saved the United States from British-style socialism, they did not prevent the invasion of Keynesian economics. John Maynard Keynes revealed his distrust of individual economic freedom in his famous *General Theory of Employment, Interest and Money* (1936): "It is certain that the world will not much longer tolerate the unemployment which, apart from brief intervals of excitement, is associated—and, in my opinion, inevitably associated—with present-day capitalistic individualism."[18]

Socialists have always believed that economic planning by politicians and bureaucrats is the surest path to growth and development. Keynesians are not socialists, but they too believe in central planning. A basic tenet of Keynesianism is an open-ended commitment to pursue full employment with budget deficits and debt. The Keynesians who dominated economic policy after the war believed, wrote Thatcher, "that the state, if its huge powers were directed in an enlightened manner, could break free of the constraints and limits which applied to the lives of individuals, families or businesses."[19]

The contribution of this doctrine to the "British disease" cannot be underestimated. "Primarily under the influence of Keynes," wrote Thatcher, "but also of socialism, the emphasis during those years was on the ability of government to improve economic conditions by direct and constant intervention."[20] Keynesian economics was not "the path to prosperity and full employment," as advertised, but the "road to ruin," she observed.[21] "Theorists of Socialism[,] … motivated by a genuine desire for social justice, elevated the State as an instrument of social regeneration," Thatcher said in 1979. "Simultaneously, Keynes and later various schools of neo-Keynesian economists, exalted the role of Government and humbled the role of the individual in their pursuit of economic stability and prosperity."[22]

Keynes was known to be hostile to classical liberalism. He insisted in a 1926 essay, "The End of Laissez-Faire," "It is *not* true that individuals possess a prescriptive 'natural liberty' in their economic activities."[23] With one foot firmly planted in Nonconformist Victorian values (his grandfather was a Nonconformist minister), he was a Liberal who supported collectivism. He was the type of Liberal, in fact, that drove Alfred Roberts out of the Liberal Party. "I criticize doctrinaire State Socialism," Keynes wrote, "not because it seeks to engage men's altruistic impulses in the service of Society, or because it departs from *laissez-faire*, or because it takes away from man's natural liberty to make a million, or because it has courage for bold experiments. All these things I applaud."[24]

Keynes's views spread from Cambridge, England, to Cambridge, Massachusetts, in 1936 with the publication of *The General Theory of Employment, Interest and Money*. The Harvard economists who digested Keynes's theories then brought them to Washington and the Roosevelt administration. Many members of Congress latched onto Keynes's ideas, particularly after the war, however unlikely it is that many of them actually read the abstruse *General Theory*. Enchanted by the Keynesian promise of government's economic omnipotence, Congress passed legislation committing the federal government to promoting growth and full employment. No politician ever wants to go before the voters with rising unemployment, so attempts to manage the economy along Keynesian lines became bipartisan in Britain and America. By the early 1970s, it could be said, "We are all Keynesians now."

One of the most popular economists of the 1950s and 1960s, John Kenneth Galbraith, expressed the complacent confidence of the Keynesians of the Great Society era in his essay, "How Keynes Came to America": "It is a measure of how far the Keynesian Revolution has proceeded that the central thesis of *The General Theory* now sounds rather commonplace."[25] Liberals had framed the debate, Galbraith noted, in such a way that "[n]obody could say that he preferred massive unemployment to Keynes."[26] On both sides of the Atlantic, it was now government's job to produce full employment and economic growth.

The problem was that as the 1970s jumped from one economic crisis to another, buffeted by inflation, unemployment, and declining output, traditional Keynesian economic policies were not working in Britain or America. A Conservative or Labour, Republican or Democratic administration could spend, run budget deficits, print money, manipulate taxes, build bridges and highways, increase welfare, and so on—just as the Ivy League and Oxbridge Keynesians recommended—but unemployment continued to rise, and economic growth faltered, leaving only inflation.

A new economic phenomenon was slowly finding its way into textbooks in the 1970s—simultaneous high inflation and unemployment. This combination, which most Keynesian economists thought could not happen, gave rise to a new term, "stagflation"—that is, stagnant economic growth accompanied by inflation. The old theory held that inflation occurred only at full employment, not before everyone was working and the economy was running at full speed. Before stagflation, it was believed there was little cost to be paid for government ensuring full employment, and that any inflation was a welcome side effect of government intervention in the economy. The term "stagflation" was actually coined in 1965 by Iain Macleod, a Conservative Member of Parliament and future Chancellor of the Exchequer.[27] The prescient Macleod first witnessed the phenomenon of incomes rising *faster* than national output a decade earlier in Britain, which signaled slower growth, rising unemployment, and inflation ahead.

Inflation, in particular, appeared uncontrollable by the 1970s. From the mid-1960s to the late 1970s, British and American economic planners were guided by the Phillips curve, devised in 1958 by the London School of Economics professor A. W. Phillips. His simple thesis was based on the empirical observation that there was a historical trade-off between inflation and unemployment. As an economy reached full employment, rising wages pushed up prices through added costs to businesses. In turn, rising wages increased demand for goods and services, which placed upward pressure on consumer prices. The Keynesians called these inflationary pressures "cost-push" and "demand-pull," respectively. The effect of sliding along the Phillips curve was that politicians and bureaucrats, intoxicated by a theory that said budget deficits and debt were good for a country, kept a watchful eye on unemployment and tried to fine-tune the economy through tax and spending policies.

By the 1970s, neither the Phillips curve nor Keynesian theory was working as expected: high inflation and unemployment were living comfortably side by side. There was no way for governments to create jobs through Keynesian policies without inviting even more inflation, which was hurting everyone. These policies were no longer associated with prosperity and full employment but with stagflation.

There was a scramble for new theories and policies. Consider, for example, the most influential American economics textbook of all time, revised from the 1940s onward, Paul Samuelson's *Economics*. Generations of American students were reared on this Keynesian classic. Samuelson wrote, "What differentiates modern inflation from that of the past is this: Prices and wages begin to rise *before* any identifiable point of full employment; *before* tight labor markets and full-capacity utilization is reached."[28] In other words: stagflation. Neither monetary nor fiscal policy, Samuelson concluded, was adequate to prevent stagflation.

In Britain, "stop-go driving"—slowing down the economy to control inflation or stimulating it to lower unemployment, based on the Phillips curve—had "proved ineffective in controlling inflation," Samuelson wrote, "and ... exacted a cruel price in terms of productivity and living standards."[29] He did not mention socialism or that Keynesian theory might have been wrong in the first place.

In the final analysis, Samuelson, like Beveridge, distrusted freedom. Full employment, price stability, and free markets were simply incompatible, he thought. Samuelson and the younger economists trained with his textbook never even considered classical liberal economic theory or lessons from the nineteenth century as alternatives to muddled Keynesian ideas. Indeed, they mocked them.

The Keynesians refused to trust the market system—in which demand and supply for goods and services determine wages and prices—to prevent greedy people from wanting more money, goods, or services. Only the government possessed the power to control avarice (or monopolize it), politicians and bureaucrats believed at the time. And why should they not have believed in this restriction on freedom, since it bestowed greater power on them? No one considered the microeconomic effects of government intervention in every market, or the obvious impracticality of trying to control wages and prices at the industry level without a substantial loss of freedom, or older theories such as the effect of the money supply on inflation. For Britain in particular, these problems had to wait until Margaret Thatcher became prime minister.

In the United States, the Nixon administration imposed wage and price controls in August 1971, an unprecedented extension of the coercive powers of government during peacetime.[30] The Heath government in Britain followed suit in November 1972, freezing prices, wages, rents, and dividends. Politicians and bureaucrats were now running the economy at a level of detail unprecedented even during war. "Politicians meeting in the Treasury decided the levels for plumbers' rates, taxi fares, and the rents on furnished versus unfurnished flats," writes Andrew Roberts.[31] Spying on one's fellow citizens was also encouraged: "Every customer was invited to be a nark, reporting shopkeepers who sneaked so much as a penny on to a can of beans."[32]

Central economic planning is frustrated not only by market activity beyond its control but also by unforeseen events. The Arab-Israeli war of 1973 was one such surprise. The Arab oil embargo that followed the

Israeli victory sent energy prices soaring and aggravated the problem of stagflation.

Imposing wage and price controls to treat inflation was as effective as bleeding a patient to treat pneumonia. It was time to rewrite the textbooks. As Thatcher explained in her memoirs:

> After decades during which governments fine-tuned the economy on the assumption that there was a "trade-off" between inflation and unemployment—the so-called Phillips Curve—it is now widely agreed that in the long run it is micro-economic changes, affecting the structure of the economy—for example, deregulation—rather than macroeconomic manipulation, which determines the number of jobs. And hardly anyone now professes to believe that "some" inflation is economically desirable.[33]

Controlling Inflation Does Not Mean Less Freedom

Critics on the Left often use the terms "Thatcherism" and "monetarism" in the same breath, and Margaret Thatcher deeply admired the principal advocate of monetarism, Milton Friedman. She credited the Nobel Laureate with having "revived the economics of liberty when it had been all but forgotten."[34]

Monetarism rejects the Keynesian notion that government can manage short-term economic growth and long-term price stability through fiscal policy (spending and taxation). For monetarists, "money matters." A predictable monetary policy is central to long-term economic growth and stable prices.

When inflation raged in the 1970s, monetarists and others pointed to monetary policy as the culprit. The Keynesians, by contrast, pointed to incomes and the need for wage and price controls. They cared about the money supply only when people had too much in their pockets. All Keynesian roads were leading to incomes policies by the 1970s.

While the theoretical debate between the monetarists and Keynesians fills volumes, at its most basic level, it is a debate about freedom. Monetarists see that heavy-handed fiscal policies, such as high taxes or wage and price controls enforced by politicians and bureaucrats, are not an effective way to "manage" the economy, while the Keynesians ignore the destructive effects of irresponsible monetary policy. In their rush to maintain full employment, they forget about the virtues of stable prices. As Thatcher reminded the British Chambers of Commerce in January 1979, inflation is not a difficult concept to understand, and controlling it does not require draconian assaults on freedom:

> One of the problems with economists these days is that they really do clothe simple propositions with really rather extravagant jargon to make them sound very much cleverer than they are. It simply means that if you pay more money or mint more money than is warranted by the production of goods and services the currency will be debased. And if I might say so, there's nothing new about that, rulers have been doing it for years, Diocletian started it in 300 A.D. and he started to replace the silver in the coinage with copper. He then got difficulties. He then was the first person who tried to impose a wages and prices policy, he had some thousand regulations about it, and then he said: I shall have one hand tied behind my back unless I have sanctions. Well there's nothing new in this but he had real tough sanctions, he said, death or deportation. You'll be glad to hear that the policy even with those sanctions proved totally unenforceable. Oh, he got the prices

controlled all right, trouble is he got them controlled at such a level that no one produced the goods.[35]

The Bankruptcy of Britain

By the 1970s the combination of socialism and Keynesian economics was destroying the British economy. Great Britain's problems were more serious than America's because socialism was far more entrenched there. While Britain headed toward bankruptcy, opposition to the policies that were bringing the country to its knees was still confined to a small group of individuals, including Thatcher.

Iain Macleod had predicted Britain's economic calamity in November 1965. "We now have the worst of both worlds—not just inflation on the one side or stagnation on the other, but both of them together," he lamented.[36] "We have a sort of 'stagflation' situation and history in modern terms is indeed being made."[37] He continued:

> There is another point behind the figures. As I say, production has fallen by 1 per cent, or ½ per cent, while incomes have gone up, perhaps, by 8 per cent. This can result only in two things happening in the months ahead; either a considerable increase in our import bill to meet the increased consumer expenditure or a very real rise in our prices. But what the First Secretary is trying to do is to conceal the rises that are likely to take place.
>
> London bus and train fares were to rise, so the Government provided a £51½ million subsidy, which runs out at the end of the year—but what then? Coal prices were to rise, so the Government gave a £15 million subsidy, which runs out in April—but what then? I ask, because all that is happening is that one is building a dam that is bound to burst in an economy where incomes are swiftly rising while production is completely stagnant.[38]

A decade later, the British government faced a severe financial crisis. No country, Macleod had warned, can go on forever subsidizing industries with declining output and productivity while maintaining the welfare state through deficit spending. In 1965, taxes paid for four-fifths of the British government's spending; that figure had fallen to three-quarters a decade later. The remainder was borrowed.[39] Like the United States today, the British government was spending more than it was taking in. During the 1970s, government spending reached a high of 50 percent of GDP.[40]

By 1976, Britain was in its worst financial shape since just after World War II. This time there was no Hitler forcing the country to spend all its wealth in a heroic struggle for survival. The damage was self-inflicted. Despair set in. James Callaghan, one of the architects of socialist Britain, supposedly told his Labour Party colleagues shortly before he became prime minister, "If I were a young man, I should emigrate."[41]

Unable to control spending, Harold Wilson resigned and was replaced as prime minister by Callaghan in March 1976. By September the government had turned to the International Monetary Fund to avert a run on the pound sterling.[42] IMF bureaucrats descended on London, ordering large spending cuts and demanding that the government control the money supply as a condition for a loan. The *Sun* carried the headline "Britain's Shame."[43] In a blow to British sovereignty, the IMF was running the country's economy. The national humiliation gave Thatcher her opportunity. "[S]ocialism as an economic doctrine," she argued, "was totally discredited."[44]

Keynesianism, Socialism, Insurrection, and Mob Violence

From the safety of faculty clubs and tenured positions, economists like Paul Samuelson proposed income policies to perfect the Phillips curve, but getting workers to cooperate could be disastrous and violent.

It is "a simple truth," wrote Samuelson, "that no jury of competent economists can reach broad agreement on how to recommend a feasible and optimal incomes policy."[45] But a jury of economists was not needed in Britain—unions already considered themselves judge, jury, and executioner. Labor unrest came to a head in late 1978 and early 1979, a season of fearsome cold and union strikes now remembered as Britain's "Winter of Discontent."

The first chill of the Winter of Discontent came in September with a strike over pay at the Ford plant at Dagenham, Essex. The automobile company capitulated, violating the Labour government's policy of holding pay increases to 5 percent. The Ford union got 17 percent.[46] The Ford strike opened the floodgates, and other strikes followed in both the private and public sectors. With inflation averaging 13 percent a year,[47] holding pay increases to 5 percent was politically impossible.

The worst strikes were by the transport union, whose truck and tanker drivers deprived the country of fuel and other vital goods. During 1979, Britain lost almost thirty million working days to strikes.[48] Public employees, whose wages chronically lagged behind those of the private sector, saw the huge concessions by companies like Ford and targeted essential services for strikes. Hospital staff, water and sanitation workers, and garbage collectors went on strike. Many National Health Service hospitals were only treating emergency patients—if a person were lucky enough to get to a hospital, for ambulance drivers were also on strike.

Unaccustomed to political resistance, the unions failed to gauge public sentiment and quickly overreached. Television cameras captured one thuggish striker at a hospital saying, "[I]f people died, so be it."[49] Gravediggers refused to bury the dead in Liverpool and Manchester, leaving decomposing bodies in hospital wards.[50] Bureaucrats were tasked to investigate if families could dig graves themselves. In the end it was concluded, "Very few people could personally dig a grave because they would have neither the skill nor the strength." The plan was abandoned.[51] When garbage collectors in the capital went on strike, mountains of rat-infested trash accumulated in Leicester Square, which beleaguered Londoners began calling "Fester Square."

Prime Minister Callaghan considered declaring a state of emergency and bringing in troops to deliver essential goods and services and restore order, but he was indecisive.[52] Provoking a confrontation between the military and the unions, Labour's chief source of political and financial support, would have been a catastrophe for the party. Callaghan, who had fought against reforms to make unions more accountable in the 1960s, appeared out of touch.[53] When he returned to London in January 1979 tanned and relaxed after a conference in the Caribbean, he was welcomed with mocking headlines: "Crisis? What Crisis?"[54]

Union membership in Britain peaked in 1979 at 13.2 million.[55] Nationalization and the growth of government had swollen the ranks of the public employee unions after 1945. The National Union of Public Employees (NUPE), which was behind much of the turmoil during the Winter of Discontent, increased from 265,000 members in 1968 to 712,000 in 1978.[56] As union strength increased, so did the influence of the radical Left. The leadership of the National Union of Mineworkers and the Transport and General Workers' Union, for example, was unabashedly Communist during the 1970s and 1980s, inspired by the Soviet Union.

The 1970s were the high-water mark of union power. They could challenge Parliamentary democracy and even force an election. In 1974, they brought down a Conservative government that had tried to tame them, and by the end of the decade, they were willing to turn on the Labour Party.

The prelude to the Winter of Discontent came after the Conservatives, led by Edward Heath, won a surprise victory over Harold Wilson's Labour government on June 18, 1970. Unlike Thatcher, Heath was never personally popular with voters, and he mistakenly believed that he could quiet the restive unions that Wilson had failed to tame. The unrest began with the dockworkers in July 1970 and spread quickly. Heath declared a national emergency, operating in a state of panic.

Heath tried to negotiate, cajole, bully, and bribe union bosses and members but to no effect. Some key union leaders liked Heath,[57] but they knew that the Labour Party was *their* party, and they saw no reason to compromise. When Heath proposed tough measures, unions took to the streets and the picket lines, believing they could win. They sensed weakness in their opponents, and they were correct.

In 1972 the coal miners went on strike for the first time in nearly fifty years, forcing power cuts throughout the country. Other unions joined in support. When the Arab oil embargo hit in 1973, life became miserable for millions. The government responded with the Keynesian sledgehammer of wage and price controls, the only effect of which was angering the unions. Many Britons faced Christmas 1973 in darkness and cold, and the chaos persisted into the new year.

The miners would not compromise, insisting on more than a 30-percent pay increase in 1974, and Heath called an election in February of that year. He framed the election as a choice between government by the unions, especially the coal miners' union, or by the Parliament. The nation returned a slim Labour majority to Parliament, which was reconfirmed in another election in October.

The Conservatives had begun edging in the right direction by 1970, calling for lower taxes and spending, moving away from nationalization, getting tough with the unions, and promoting free enterprise—bucking Britain's postwar consensus. But Heath did not have the courage or resolve to see it through. He lacked the stomach for the type of fight that Thatcher would relish.

Heath's only lasting contribution to economic policy was joining the Common Market (the forerunner of the European Union), the great cause of his political career since the Macmillan government. He hoped that the better-performing economies in Europe, particularly West Germany, would force Britain through greater European integration to be more competitive. In many ways it was like the IMF forcing the British to improve their finances and practice monetary and fiscal restraint. Politicians and bureaucrats seemed incapable of reversing economic decline and needed help from abroad. No one, it seemed, was committed to fundamental changes in economic policy.[58] Margaret Thatcher, however, was waiting in the wings.

Key Leadership Lessons

- Do not be afraid to challenge conventional wisdom and deeply entrenched ways of thinking. Thatcher offered a compelling, commonsense alternative to socialist and Keynesian dogma.

- The road to British economic ruin in the 1970s was paved with big-government solutions. Conservatives must ensure that America takes a different path.

- Never assume that government knows best when it comes to economic success. Thatcher trusted the instincts of entrepreneurs and small business owners and was wary of following the advice of bureaucrats and heads of government-owned industries.

- Be prepared to stand up to the power of organized labor, which often acts as a barrier to economic freedom and growth. Never give in to attempts by unions to intimidate workers or to undermine the rule of law or the democratic process.

CHAPTER FOUR

THE THATCHER REVOLUTION

*"I set out to destroy socialism because I felt it was
at odds with the character of the people. We were the first country
in the world to roll back the frontiers of socialism,
then roll forward the frontiers of freedom."*
—MARGARET THATCHER, "DON'T UNDO MY WORK,"
NEWSWEEK, APRIL 27, 1992[1]

The Rise to Conservative Party Leader

Edward Heath had to go as Conservative Party leader. He had been in Parliament since 1950, and he climbed the greasy pole to chief whip, Conservative Party leader, and finally prime minister. But he was not a vote magnet or even a particularly appealing politician, as his three losses in four general elections demonstrated.

On November 25, 1974, Margaret Thatcher entered Heath's office. She had made one of the greatest decisions of her life: to challenge him for leadership of the Conservative Party. The exchange was brief. She said, "I must tell you that I have decided to stand for the leadership." Heath turned his back on her and replied, "If you must."[2] With that clipped exchange, the Thatcher era began.

Thatcher's ministerial service had begun under Harold Macmillan as an undersecretary for pensions and national insurance. A decade later she served loyally in Heath's cabinet, fighting thankless public relations battles on his behalf as the secretary of state for education and science. The government's attempt to apply means tests to the distribution of free milk in schools led to taunts of "Mrs. Thatcher, milk snatcher."[3]

The pensions and education posts taught Thatcher how the welfare state worked. She believed that politicians and other public officials had to master their briefs and meet their administrative responsibilities. Excellence in public service was as important as political victory to her. Inattention to detail, neglect of her work, and ineffective administration were inconceivable to Margaret Thatcher. As her early promotion in government (a mere two years after winning her seat in Parliament) showed, her intelligence, drive, and competence attracted attention from the beginning of her career.

The debacle of the Heath government forced many in the Conservative Party to rethink their purpose. What did they stand for? Trying to govern like Keynesians and socialists was a political disaster. According to Thatcher, the Heath government "proposed and almost implemented the most radical form of socialism ever contemplated by an elected British Government."[4] Yet Conservatives had nothing to show for it.

The only question in 1974 was whether anyone would have the courage to challenge Heath for the leadership and change the direction of the party. It was one thing for the Conservative establishment to complain about their leader over brandy and cigars at the Carlton Club. It was quite another to step forward and mount a challenge, knowing that failure meant an end to one's political career. The challenge, when it came, was from outside the establishment.

After the Tories' defeat in February 1974, Thatcher and her mentor, the brilliant Sir Keith Joseph, were the first prominent Conservatives to challenge the party's economic policies since Macmillan and its adherence to consensus politics since 1945. As Thatcher wrote in her memoirs, the Tories, at best, "loosened the corset of socialism; they never removed it."[5] Thatcher's own choice to challenge Heath after the October 1974 general election was Joseph, who ultimately became the Tory Moses to Thatcher's Joshua. The former led his people out of bondage to the establishment, but it was left for the latter to conquer and settle the promised land.

Joseph had great intellectual courage, but he could stumble into needless controversy. Thatcher's political instincts, by contrast, rarely failed her. When, in a speech at Birmingham, Joseph discussed certain self-destructive social pathologies among the lower classes in a way that was easily misconstrued, he quickly decided that he was not the candidate to lead the Conservative Party. So the cup passed to Margaret Thatcher.

The Conservative establishment rallied around Heath, just as establishment Republicans would rally around Gerald Ford the following year when he faced a challenge from Ronald Reagan. As an early supporter of Thatcher, Jock Bruce-Gardyne, observed, the establishment "tolerated" Heath, who came from an undistinguished family, "rather as their forebears had tolerated Disraeli: not one of them, of course, but prepared to learn, and the best advocate for the cause who happened to be currently available."[6] They viewed Thatcher with unmasked suspicion because she was a conviction politician and unwilling to bow before them. She became the target of malicious and absurd rumors. These attacks, she later wrote, "showed many people from modest backgrounds like mine how close to the surface of the Tory grandees lay an ugly streak of contempt for those they considered voting fodder."[7]

Challenging Heath required considerable political courage. At first, she thought she could not win but believed a challenge to Heath was imperative, particularly after Joseph backed down. Her husband told her, "You must be out of your mind. You haven't got a hope."[8] She knew that if Heath won reelection as leader, "I was politically finished."[9] Conservative rank-and-file unease, however, proved far more widespread than many Conservative leaders in Parliament thought. Heath's U-turns and his disastrous handling of the economy had been humiliating for many of them, including Thatcher.

In a column published in the *Daily Telegraph* just before the leadership election, Thatcher acknowledged her share of responsibility as a cabinet member for the failures of the Heath government—something Heath and his allies were incapable of doing. This acknowledgment, she said, required a new vision for the Conservative Party. "My kind of Tory party," Thatcher wrote, "would make no secret of its belief in individual freedom and individual prosperity, in the maintenance of law and order, in the wide distribution of private property, in rewards for energy, skill and thrift, in diversity of choice, in the preservation of local rights in local communities."[10] The reasons for the Conservative defeats in 1974, she added, were not difficult to see. "Indeed one of the reasons for our electoral failure is that people believe too many Conservatives *have* become socialists already. Britain's progress towards socialism has been an alternation of two steps forward with half a step back. ... And why should anyone support a party that seems to have the courage of no convictions?"[11]

Thatcher beat the odds and defeated Heath for the leadership in February 1975. Enough Conservative MPs were fed up with Heath, and her courage, conviction, and organization were clear to all. Her challenge to Heath was honest and straightforward—there was nothing knife-in-the-back about it. Heath may have sulked for years, but there would never be any doubt that he had been beaten fair and square.

The Battle for Downing Street

In a country facing uncontrollable inflation, rising unemployment, and union chaos, leading a major political party was unimaginably challenging.

It did not seem to matter whether it was Edward Heath, Harold Wilson, or James Callaghan at the helm; the country could not escape being the sick man of Europe. By 1979, a different type of leader was needed to break the postwar mold.

Socialism and Keynesianism were so deeply entrenched that continued economic decline seemed inevitable. Free people, however, have the power to change their path—*if* they have leaders of conviction. Beginning in the Winter of Discontent, Margaret Thatcher changed the model of British leadership. She not only knew what had to be done; she understood the British people as well. Unlike many in the Conservative establishment, she believed that the great achievements of the past were based on the character of the people and were an indication of what was possible for the future. How many leaders in history have been unable to seize the moment because they failed to inspire the people or lacked courage? We can only speculate what would have happened to Britain without Winston Churchill or Margaret Thatcher.

The changes in British politics that are now taken for granted were by no means inevitable in 1975. Thatcher had allies but was also the consummate outsider who had stepped forward when others had hesitated or miscalculated. She therefore had rivals and enemies. Virulent (and violent) opposition from socialists and unions was, of course, expected. But there were also other ambitious Tories who would have liked to replace Heath. They watched carefully for any missteps by the party's new leader. Thatcher eventually won the reliable support of the party faithful around the country, but the backing of the Conservative establishment always remained shaky. They looked on Thatcher "as little better than an aberration," wrote Bruce-Gardyne. If she had failed to lead in 1979, she would have been shown the door quickly, for the queue to replace her was not short.[12]

Thatcher realized early in the Winter of Discontent that she had to be bold. Union bosses would never accept measures to make them more accountable or support anti-inflationary policies, no matter how many beers and sandwiches they were served at 10 Downing Street—an unsuccessful tactic Harold Wilson and Edward Heath had used to win over union leaders. (A miner once complained, "The beer was not very cold and the sandwiches were so dry they were turned up at the edges.")[13] Compromise was no longer an option, though many across the political spectrum hoped for it—a hope that the union bosses easily exploited. As a cabinet minister in the Heath government, Thatcher had witnessed firsthand what unions were prepared to do to bring down a Conservative government. Now they were confronting *their own* political party in a similar manner. Compromise with such ruthless groups would have been viewed as a white flag.

Other veterans of Heath's government were reluctant to challenge the unions or the established economic policies. Norman St. John-Stevas, a Tory MP, had declared in 1976, "No Government in Britain can hope to succeed today without the good will of the unions."[14] This view was not shared by Thatcher, who vowed in an interview in 1979, "By God I'll confront them."[15] Tories who had been traumatized by union power from 1970 to 1974 urged her to adopt a less confrontational approach and side with the government on their incomes policy.[16] Even during the Winter of Discontent and afterward, they urged their leader not to be "too insensitive or controversial," insisting that "there had to be a third way"; for if she "told the truth about the unions we should certainly lose the election."[17] Thatcher knew, however, that she had the British people with her in 1979. "Personally, I was conscious that in some strange way I was instinctively speaking and feeling in harmony with the great majority of the population," she wrote. "Such moments are as unforgettable as they are rare. They must be seized to change history."[18]

Great leaders understand trepidation among supporters and allies, as well as the weakness of enemies. They know they have to inspire, win support, and, when necessary, quell unrest within their own ranks. In 1979, when the dead were going unburied and union thugs were stopping sick people from entering hospitals, Thatcher realized there was no turning back. Patriotism alone should have aroused Conservative anger. The unions were tormenting the British people, many of whom had fought two World Wars, suffered tremendous economic hardships, and supported socialism hoping for a better future, which never came. Thatcher expressed the indignation of all British patriots. Jim Prior, her shadow minister for employment, who was urging moderation in 1979, came to realize that Thatcher was "much more in tune with the people"[19] than he and the other timid Conservatives were.

The Winter of Discontent demonstrated that the Labour Party was weak and no longer operated in the interest of the country. This was the moment when Thatcher became the spokeswoman for Britain's "silent majority," the ordinary men and women who provided for their families, educated their children, gave life to churches and communities, and loved their country.

Thatcher had three objectives. First, she had to challenge the government over economic policy and appeasement of unions. Second, she had to win the public over to her side for strong action against unions and for ending Britain's ruinous economic policies. Third, she had to win a vote of no confidence against the Labour government, force a general election, and win. None of these would be easy to achieve, and realizing all three appeared nearly impossible.

Thatcher began by rallying the country to confront the unions and reverse its economic decline. On television, in the House of Commons, and on the hustings, her performances were legendary. She stressed that the unions—under the control of the radical Left and unappeasable—had to be subjected to the rule of law. The rank and file, she insisted, had a right to a secret ballot on strike votes. Picketing should be restricted, peaceful, and lawful. The closed shop should be reformed, and essential services should never be halted by strikes. She argued that the Labour Party, controlled as it was by the union bosses, was incapable of making these reforms. Labour had traditionally campaigned on its ability to manage the unions, but by the 1970s, this boast had become a bad joke.

In an interview on the widely watched television program *Weekend World* a few months before the 1979 general election, Thatcher argued that the debate before the country was about union power in a democracy, and she launched an assault on Keynesian incomes policies, which had brought the economy to the verge of collapse.[20]

A few days later, on the floor of the House of Commons, Thatcher pounded away at a Callaghan government on the ropes. The Labour Party was incapable of resolving industrial disputes, she said, because it had a history of encouraging strikes in concert with union bosses as an opposition tactic against Conservative governments. Their irresponsibility had come back to haunt them, especially now that the unions were at the height of their power and increasingly dominated by radical leftists. Not only had the government lost control of the unions, but many union bosses were also losing control over their members. She said that the "time of mounting power for the trade unions has also been a period when we have seen increasing Left-wing militancy in control of the unions."[21] In particular, she cited the transport strike, led by the Transport and General Workers' Union, one of the severest hardships of the Winter of Discontent. "[O]ne of the reasons that this strike was made official," she said, "was that it was already out of control. It went out of control because of the mounting Left-Wing nature of that union."[22]

A televised Conservative political advertisement the next day gave her the opportunity to make her case to the British public during prime time. Plainly dressed and seated in a chair in her room in Parliament, Thatcher rose above political turmoil and reminded the nation of its greatness. She may not have been the most beloved leader in British history at that point, but her countrymen knew they could bank on what she said—a rare quality in any politician.

Thatcher made it clear she did not want to score political points. "The crisis that our country faces is too serious for that," she said. "And it is our country, the whole nation, that faces this crisis, not just one party or even one government. This is no time to put party before country. I start from there."[23] Great leaders in the middle of a crisis always appeal to the better angels of their countrymen. Thatcher reminded her audience what a privilege it was to live in Britain. The country would survive union unrest and socialism, but its belief in a better future had to be restored. This address stands as the testimony of a great patriot:

> Despite our problems and our failures this is still a good land to live in and bring up a family. It is a land of great natural riches—the coal beneath our feet, the oil and gas in the sea around our shores, the fertile acres of our farms. It is also a land of great human resources. We still have—we have always had—enterprise and skills, firms and industries whose workers can perform as well as any in the world.
>
> What we do not have are the right conditions, the incentive for success. It is this incentive we must and can create. But to do so we must first stop tearing ourselves apart.
>
> If the present crisis has taught us anything it has surely taught us that we have to think of others as well as ourselves; that no-one, however strong his case, is entitled to pursue it by hurting others.
>
> There are wreckers among us who don't believe this. But the vast majority of us, and that includes the vast majority of

trade unionists, do believe it, whether we call ourselves Labour, Conservative, Liberal—or simply British.

It is to that majority that I am talking this evening. We have to learn again to be one nation, or one day we shall be no nation. If we have learnt that lesson from these first dark days of 1979, then we have learnt something of value.[24]

It is easy to talk about cooperating in a campaign speech, but Thatcher went a step further. In the House of Commons and in that televised speech, she offered to work with the Callaghan government to bring forward legislation to reform the unions. "We believe that this is a matter of great significance for democracy and a free society," she said in the House, "and we will support him if he will take steps to deal with these problems."[25]

This was a risky offer. If accepted, it would extend the life of a failed government, promising more socialism and union unrest. While it was always unlikely that Callaghan would accept the offer, it gave him an opportunity to take away an issue that was gaining traction for the Conservatives. Callaghan saluted her statesmanship in the House of Commons: "I congratulate the right honorable Lady on a most effective parliamentary performance. It was in the best manner of our debates and the style in which it was delivered was one of which the right honorable Lady can be proud."[26]

As January gave way to February, no one believed that the militancy of the unions or the country's other economic problems were ending. The Winter of Discontent would be only a taste of things to come if the unions were not brought under control and economic policies not dramatically changed. It was time for the Labour government to be consigned to history. Thatcher began preparing a no-confidence motion in March to force an election. It turned out to be high drama indeed.

The Labour government, which had lacked a majority since 1977, had compiled a record of economic mismanagement (building, it must be said, on Heath's foundations) unmatched in British history. It limped along in a coalition with the Liberal Party and cooperated with regional parties in Scotland, Wales, and Northern Ireland, who were promised greater autonomy (which they never received) in exchange for their support. The government itself, held together with tape, string, and broken promises, seemed to reflect the disintegration of Britain in the 1970s. Thatcher was able to peel off enough government supporters to force a vote of confidence. If the vote went in favor of the government, Callaghan would have a much-needed victory and Thatcher's Tory enemies would be emboldened: "A Government victory would strengthen it at a bad time."[27]

The vote was taken on March 28, 1979. By the narrowest of margins—311 to 310—the House of Commons forced an election. As Thatcher recalled, "So at last I had my chance, my only chance. I must seize it with both hands."[28]

A British campaign season is mercifully short. The general election was held on May 3, 1979, giving the Conservatives a healthy forty-three-seat majority. As Thatcher proclaimed during the heat of the campaign, "Change is coming. The slither and slide to the socialist state is going to be stopped in this United Kingdom of Great Britain and Northern Ireland, stopped, halted and turned back [applause]. It can be done, it will be done, and we intend to make a start on the 4th May."[29]

She appealed to history. "But the changes we propose are securely rooted in the old and trusted values that have held a great nation together in the past and served her well. Tennyson said, 'That man's the true conservative who lops the mouldered branch away'. For us the Socialism of recent years in Britain with its terrible emphasis on state power, with its class prejudice, with its facile Marxist labels which have no connection with our real world, for us all that is the mouldered branch which should be lopped away."[30]

One of Thatcher's core convictions, which always gave her the confidence to pursue change, was that socialism never really had a home in British hearts. In her last broadcast to the country before the election, she said, "I've never believed that this country is a naturally socialist country. We're an independent people; we don't take easily to having more and more of our lives decided for us by the State. We don't take kindly to being pushed around."[31] But socialism had marred the British spirit. "Many of our troubles stem from the fact that in recent years we haven't been true to ourselves; true to our tradition of independence—largely because we've been encouraged not to be."[32]

The implications of Thatcher's victory that May were not lost on American conservatives at the time. It boosted Ronald Reagan's prospects because the United States and Britain faced many of the same problems. William F. Buckley Jr. emphasized the historic nature of Thatcher's victory in his newspaper column: "this one *was* truly vital, and everyone who voted for Thatcher should be as proud as if he had fought on St. Crispin's Day."[33] The election had proved that socialism was not inevitable and could be stopped. "The British had reached the point where all the conventional nostrums of socialism had been explored"—and failed.[34] "Evelyn Waugh complained that the trouble with our century is that we never succeeded in turning the clock back a single second," wrote Buckley. "The voters may now have proved him wrong."[35] The day before the election, Buckley wired Thatcher: "I and what's left of the free world rooting for you, love."[36]

Putting the Great Back into Britain

In November 1988, over twenty thousand Poles loudly cheered Thatcher when she met Lech Walesa, the leader of Solidarity, the union that helped to bring down communism in Poland, at the fabled Lenin Shipyard. No British leader had received such applause since Winston Churchill. The Poles knew what the Iron Lady had done to roll back socialism in Britain and how it gave hope to the millions of victims of socialism in Eastern Europe. Thatcherism had triumphed while socialism was falling apart everywhere.

From the moment Margaret Thatcher entered Edward Heath's office on November 25, 1974, the course of history was changed. After her death, Mikhail Gorbachev wrote, "I recall vividly her first visit to the USSR in spring 1987. She amazed me by her knowledge of our domestic developments, her understanding of the nature of changes then under way, her ability to evaluate them realistically and her readiness *to share with us the experience* of what she called 'my own perestroika.'"[37] Thatcher's "own perestroika" was rolling back socialism in Britain, which provided a model for the Soviet Union and Eastern Europe. "I set out to destroy socialism because I felt it was at odds with the character of the people," she wrote in 1992. "We were the first country in the world to roll back the frontiers of socialism, then roll forward the frontiers of freedom."[38]

Thatcher's boldness was evident in her days in the Parliamentary Opposition, when she proposed measures that her detractors thought were impossible to achieve and would surely cost her the election. Socialism, they thought, was too entrenched for the type of renewal she was proposing. Praise for the virtues of the Victorian age, for example, was considered too far removed from the present to have any effect on British voters. Thatcher's opponents could only hope that voters would reject her message, personality, and policies, since they had no alternatives to her agenda other than the status quo. But the voters did not reject her—not in 1979 or 1983 or 1987. Nor did they reject her in 1992, when her party, under her successor, John Major, won a historic fourth term in office.

In 1979, Thatcher's opponents offered only two economic plans. Labour moderates, Liberals, and center-left Conservatives proposed wage and price controls, inflation, Keynesian demand management, and deepening commitment to the European Economic Community. The Labour mainstream was committed to socialism and even greater government control than had existed in the 1940s. Neither alternative resonated with a majority of the British people.

Critics looking back on Thatcher's victories have tried to denigrate her political achievements. She faced weak opposition, they say, from the Labour Party, which was embroiled in internal disputes and therefore unable to mount an effective opposition to her. The party split along ideological lines with the formation of the Social Democratic Party (SDP). Later, Labour leaders were preoccupied with purging or marginalizing the party's radical Left.

Turmoil among the socialists, however, was not the cause of Thatcher's victory, though it was a factor in her initial success. "The more the general public learned of Labour's policies and personnel the less they liked them," she wrote in her memoirs.[39] Regardless of socialism's declining appeal in the 1980s and 1990s, Thatcher warned, it "represents an enduring temptation: no one should underestimate Labour's potential appeal."[40]

Critics have further argued that the Callaghan government had already adopted an anti-inflation monetary policy and spending reductions under IMF guidance. They locate the origins of Thatcherism in policy reforms begun by Heath before the 1970 election. In other words, there was nothing unique about Thatcher, and Thatcherism's lineage includes Edward Heath and James Callaghan! This is absurd, for neither Callaghan nor Heath believed in the principles of Thatcherism. They thought the IMF and EEC would do the heavy lifting for them. Thatcherism is about British politicians doing the heavy lifting themselves.

Margaret Thatcher certainly did the heavy lifting, whereas her three predecessors did not or could not. When she became prime minister, she faced the same problems they did. Yet these problems did not consume her or force her out of office. She believed in conviction politics—knowing what works and what does not, and not confusing the two in the name of ideology or expedience. Thatcher was successful because, as she would remind people, her convictions were based on rediscovering the principles that made Britain great and contributed to freedom and prosperity everywhere. By 1979, socialism and Keynesianism had brought misery to the British people. It was time for a new course.

Margaret Thatcher and Ronald Reagan led a conservative, or neoliberal, revolution that swept the world in the 1980s. They championed the classical liberalism of Gladstone, which had reemerged after 1945, adapted to the modern world in the works of Friedrich Hayek, Milton Friedman, and other brave free-market thinkers. This revolution led to unprecedented economic prosperity, the rolling back of socialism—an ideology that had once seemed destined to dominate the world—and the ultimate prize of freedom: the end of Soviet communism. By 1990, the world was a better place for most of humanity than at any previous time in history.

The resurgence in classical liberal ideas was certainly vital in countering textbooks like Samuelson's, whose policy recommendations were becoming a guide to economic disaster. The creation in the 1970s of The Heritage Foundation in Washington, D.C., for example, heralded the rise of Ronald Reagan in the Republican party, just as the creation in London of the Centre for Policy Studies by Sir Keith Joseph heralded the rise of Margaret Thatcher in the Conservative Party.[41]

It was their passionate commitment to these ideas of freedom that distinguished Thatcher and Reagan from their predecessors of the 1970s. Edward Heath and James Callaghan in Britain and Richard Nixon and

Jimmy Carter in the United States were occasionally steered by events and politics into neoliberal reforms. But none of them cared about expanding economic freedom and limiting government the way Thatcher and Reagan did. The 1980s, as a result, were far more successful than the 1970s.

Under President Reagan, the U.S. economy enjoyed the longest peacetime expansion then on record—ninety-two months. This was followed by another long expansion with a short recession in between—an unmatched economic record.[42] Deregulation and lower taxes produced low inflation, low unemployment, and strong economic growth—a happy combination the Keynesians thought was impossible. Stagflation went the way of disco.

Thatcher's success was even more dramatic considering the depths of socialism and union militancy from which she had to rescue the British economy. Inflation was controlled through monetary policy. The disastrous incomes policy of her predecessors was "laid to rest."[43] She deregulated British businesses, especially the financial services industry, and London became one of the leading financial centers in the world again. "Sound public finances and low marginal tax rates were the goals in the 1980s," Thatcher recalled, "and they were achieved."[44]

The raging inflation that Thatcher inherited peaked at 21.9 percent in May 1980. By the summer of 1986, it was 2.4 percent, a remarkable turnaround from the previous decade.[45] Money "mattered" again in controlling prices, not negotiating with union bosses. After 1992, with inflation tamed, price stability governed the Bank of England's monetary policy. The eventual result of Thatcher's victory over runaway inflation was that in 1997 the government was able to grant the Bank of England independence in its monetary policy.

Thatcher's greatest domestic triumph, however, was rolling back socialism. By 1990, the state-owned sector had been reduced by 60 percent. After putting the old nationalized companies on a sound financial footing, Thatcher sold their shares to the public. Because of privatization and other government policies, some 25 percent of the British population were stockholders by 1990.[46]

Reform of the unions was the other step in dismantling socialism and reviving the British economy. Since the Labour government of Harold Wilson, it was well known that union actions were hurting worker productivity and the competitiveness of the British economy. By the 1980s, serious change was long overdue. Thatcher promised to deliver on union reform during the Winter of Discontent, and over the next eight years, she substantially reined in union power. The 1982 Employment Act, as her advisor Robin Harris describes it, "introduced two key changes. It gave employers the right to sue for damages, where no dispute existed with their own employees or where it was not wholly or mainly about employment matters. Most important, for the first time it exposed trade union funds to fines and seizure in the case of unlawful industrial action."[47] This was followed by the 1984 Trade Union Act, the 1988 Employment Act, and the 1990 Employment Act, which ended the union practice of the "closed shop." The measures dramatically reduced union militancy, and union membership lost much of its appeal. By 1990, the number of labor stoppages fell to levels not seen since 1935, and the number of working days lost to strikes fell to 1950s averages.[48] The percentage of the labor force in unions fell from 50 percent to 35 percent.[49]

There was one last attempt by the National Union of Mineworkers—led by an unregenerate Stalinist, Arthur Scargill[50]—to challenge the Thatcher government in 1984 and 1985. But unlike her hapless predecessors of the 1970s, Thatcher made sure the country was prepared with sufficient coal stocks to ride out the strike and enough police to ensure order around pits. Scargill and the NUM were defeated. Profitable pits were privatized, unprofitable pits were closed, and compensation was given to miners. Law and order was maintained after Scargill and his thugs resorted to violence. Scargill was unable to get broader union support from the railway or the dockworkers, key to any general strike. It was an important test of whether an elected Parliament or union bosses were going to run the country.

The miners' strike of 1984–85 was the last great strike in an era that stretched back before World War I. While twenty-seven million working days were lost to the strike in 1984, its impact was felt less by the country and more by the trade unions, which realized that Thatcher's strength lay in the success of her economic policies.[51] Her policies reversed nearly all the economic problems of the 1970s that union bosses had been able to exploit through strife and violence. Scargill even lost the support of the Labour Party. The retreat of stagflation and socialism deprived the unions of their platform, and the era of union militancy was brought to an end by 1985. The primary illness of the sick man of Europe was in remission.

By any measure, the Thatcher revolution of the late 1970s and 1980s was a staggering achievement. The British people could once again take pride in their country and hold their heads high in Europe and on the world stage. As Lady Thatcher remarked soon after leaving office, "Thatcherism will live. It will live long after Thatcher has died, because we had the courage to restore the great principles and put them into practice, in keeping with the character of the people and the place of this country in the world."[52]

Key Leadership Lessons

- Do not be deterred by early electoral defeats. Thatcher lost twice before winning a seat in Parliament. A strong leader must be prepared to face and overcome setbacks and prepare for the next battle.
- Victory always goes to the brave. Courage and a willingness to take risks are hallmarks of successful leadership. In 1979

and throughout the 1980s, Thatcher assumed great risks on behalf of the British people and was rewarded at the polls.

- Courage must be matched by conviction and the strength to stand by core beliefs and principles.

- Always take responsibility for your actions and the actions of your party, even if they may be unpopular. Conservatives must not seek to emulate the Left, either in opposition or in government, if they wish to be truly successful.

- Never be afraid to make an appeal to patriotism the heart of your message. Thatcher consistently placed love of country at the center of her leadership.

- Promoting economic freedom involves tough choices and potential unpopularity. Being the first leader in the world in the 1980s to reverse socialism required unmatched courage—and a belief that people will always choose freedom over big government if the choice is offered to them by conservatives.

CHAPTER FIVE

AMERICA MUST AVOID EUROPEAN-STYLE DECLINE

*"During my lifetime most of the problems the world
has faced have come, in one fashion or other, from
mainland Europe, and the solutions from outside it."*
—MARGARET THATCHER, *STATECRAFT: STRATEGIES
FOR A CHANGING WORLD*[1]

The Reversal of British Decline

Margaret Thatcher famously declared in a 1976 television interview, "Socialist governments traditionally do make a financial mess. They always run out of other people's money. It's quite a characteristic of them."[2] When she entered Downing Street three years later, the country was on its deathbed after several years of socialist misrule. The Labour governments of the 1970s had been "intent on distributing wealth instead of creating it, and without anything to distribute."[3] Britain, a once-great imperial power, was widely written off as a hopeless case. Economists now referred to the "British disease." It was a soul-destroying state of affairs, enough to sap the will of all but the most ardent of patriots.

It is hard to believe that a nation that once governed huge stretches of Asia, Africa, North America, and the Middle East could have been reduced to begging from the International Monetary Fund to pay its bills. Sir Winston Churchill would have been horrified. The United Kingdom was even officially classified at a meeting of the European Council in 1979 as "a less prosperous country," or "LPC,"[4] the equivalent of present-day Greece or Spain. Britain had the most oppressive tax system of any country in the free world, with the highest starting rate of tax in the European Economic Community.[5] Britain's GDP per capita ranked just seventh out of nine EEC members in 1979.[6] Output per head that year was 50 percent higher in Germany and France than in Britain.[7]

Britain's humiliating plight moved many commentators at home and abroad to pen the nation's obituary. A *Wall Street Journal* editorial in August 1975 (which appalled Margaret Thatcher at the time) scolded the British for bringing about their own decline:

> Hardly anyone needs to be told now that Great Britain is the sick country of Europe. Everywhere you look the evidence abounds. It is all very curious. For Britain has not been brought to this state by defeat in war, by earthquakes, plagues, droughts or any natural disasters. Britain's undoing is its own doing. It has been brought to this by the calculated policies of its Government and by their resigned acceptance by the people.[8]

The British people, eight million of whom were dependent on government welfare, suffered from an overwhelming lack of confidence in themselves and in their country's values. After decades of socialism, they had begun to lose faith in the very foundations of the free-enterprise system. As Thatcher put it in a speech to the Conservative Party conference in 1980, "It is not the State that creates a healthy society.... The State drains society, not only of its wealth but of initiative, of energy, the will to improve and innovate as well as to preserve what is best."[9] The nation whose entrepreneurial spirit had given birth to the Industrial Revolution, whose bankers, traders, businessmen, and adventurers had brought capitalism to every corner of the globe, was mired in public debt, regulation, heavy taxes, and oppressive trade union power.

Margaret Thatcher was determined to reverse Britain's decline. She simply would not accept that her great nation would go the way of ancient Greece or Rome. In her famous "Iron Lady" speech in 1976, three years before she became prime minister, she issued this rallying cry to her country:

> We are often told how this country that once ruled a quarter of the world is today just a group of offshore islands. Well, we in the Conservative Party believe that Britain is still great. The decline of our relative power in the world was partly inevitable—with the rise of the super powers with their vast reserves of manpower and resources.
>
> But it was partly avoidable too—the result of our economic decline accelerated by Socialism. We must reverse that decline when we are returned to Government. In the meantime, the Conservative Party has the vital task of shaking the British public out of a long sleep.[10]

It took a conservative revolution led by Thatcher to turn Britain's fortunes around. It was a revolution based on the principles of limited government, thrift, and free enterprise. It brought lower taxes, tighter fiscal discipline, cuts in government spending, the liberation of the markets, and the roll-ing back of the frontiers of the welfare state. The scale of Britain's turn-around in the 1980s was simply staggering. By 1987, Britain had enjoyed the longest sustained period of economic growth since World War II.[11] Ten thousand small businesses had been created in just the first four years of the Thatcher government.[12] Three quarters of a million new jobs were created between 1983 and 1991—more than in any other country in the EEC.[13] At the same time, Thatcher took an axe to the government bureau-cracy, cutting the number of civil servants by more than a fifth.[14]

The Thatcher revolution "brought about a profound change in the attitudes, social, political, even spiritual, of our people. They became more self-reliant, more responsible, more independent, more forward-looking. They had a stake in the future."[15] Thatcher also combined economic renewal with a strong national defense, increasing British defense spend-ing while bolstering the transatlantic alliance. She invested great energy in defending British sovereignty in Europe, which she saw as essential to maintaining Britain's prosperity as well as its ability to shape its own destiny. Her achievement in Britain was a striking demonstration of how principled leadership can turn a country around in the face of seemingly insurmountable odds. As the Iron Lady put it in 1977, before becoming prime minister, "We are not bound to an irrevocable decline. We see noth-ing as inevitable. Men can still shape history."[16]

The End of the U.S. Superpower?

There are striking parallels between the debates in Britain in the 1970s and 1980s and those taking place in the United States today. There is a palpable sense of decline across America, with a rising fear that the nation's best days are behind it. A Gallup poll conducted in January 2013, just ahead of President Obama's second inauguration, showed that "Americans are as negative about the state of the country and its prospects going forward as they have been in more than three decades. Fewer than four in ten Americans (39 percent) rate the current status of the United States at the positive end of a zero-to-ten scale. This is about the same as in 2010, but it is fewer than have said so at any point since 1979."[17] Contrast this with the optimism Americans felt in January 2001, at the beginning of the George W. Bush presidency, when 73 percent of Americans felt positive about their country's future. Or even the 50 percent of Americans with a positive outlook for America in January 2008, at the start of the last year of the Bush presidency.

America is also more deeply divided today than at any time in its recent history. Another Gallup poll, released just after the 2013 presidential inauguration, showed Barack Obama's fourth year in office tied with George W. Bush's last year in office as the most polarized since Gallup began tracking the issue during the Eisenhower administration. As Gallup notes, President Obama is well on course to becoming the most polarizing president in American history, with only 10 percent of Republicans approving of the president's record in 2012. In contrast, 24 percent of Republicans approved of Bill Clinton's performance in his fourth year in office. Even Jimmy Carter received a higher level of approval (24 percent) among Republicans in his fourth year than did Barack Obama in January 2013.[18]

It is not hard to see why most Americans are gloomy about their nation's future and why conservatives have so little faith in President Obama. Talk in Washington is dominated by discussion of America's huge debts, which almost doubled during President Obama's first term. Government spending and the budget deficit are consistently at the top of American voter concerns alongside the general state of the economy and unemployment. Concerns over unsustainable levels of debt led to the rise in 2010 of the Tea Party, undeniably the most effective grassroots movement the United States has seen in decades. Carried on a wave of Tea Party anger, the Republicans scored huge victories in the 2010 midterms, with the GOP taking the House of Representatives, giving the White House what President Obama described at the time as a "shellacking." This momentum was not enough to unseat President Obama in the 2012 presidential election, but fiscal conservatism remains a powerful force in American politics, and the issue of America's out-of-control government spending will only grow larger in Obama's second term.

Put simply, if America's economic woes are not addressed, the United States faces an exceedingly bleak economic future similar to that of Greece, France, Italy, and Spain. According to the OECD, China could overtake the United States as the world's largest economy by 2016.[19] The next few years will be critical to shaping America's path in the twenty-first century, just as the 1980s were central to British renewal. The leadership lessons of Margaret Thatcher have never been more vital for America's conservatives than they are today. Conservatives must fight with the same conviction that drove the Iron Lady in the face of what at times appeared to be almost insurmountable opposition from deeply entrenched liberal elites, an incredibly powerful trade union movement, and a frequently hostile media, not least the BBC.

The Threat of American Economic Decline

Huge national debts and spiraling budget deficits are undoubtedly the biggest challenges to America's long-term prosperity. America's position as the world's superpower is under serious threat from economic weakness at home. As in 1970s Britain, talk of decline is everywhere in American politics today. The Obama presidency has been a disastrous experiment in big government, one that has racked up the largest budget deficits since the Second World War.[20] The precedent this sets is extremely worrying. As Margaret Thatcher warned in a 1992 interview with *Newsweek*: "There is an Italian saying, 'Public spending is like holy water: everyone helps himself.' The greatest danger to government in Britain—and the United States—is having too many elected representatives who think they make their reputation or keep their seats by securing an extra chunk of public spending for their own constituency or cause. You don't judge morality in politics by how deeply you can put your hand into the taxpayer's pocket."[21]

The United States' national debt is simply stunning. At more than $16 trillion, it already exceeds 100 percent of GDP according to the OECD,[22] with publicly held debt projected to exceed 100 percent of U.S. GDP by 2024.[23] According to the Congressional Budget Office, U.S. federal debt shot up from 40 percent of GDP at the end of 2008 to more than 70 percent by the end of 2012.[24] Under the CBO's extended alternative fiscal scenario, federal debt will exceed 90 percent of GDP in 2022 and will surpass its historical peak of 109 percent by 2026, approaching 200 percent in 2037.[25] The new healthcare reforms implemented by the Obama administration, commonly known as "Obamacare" (or the Affordable Care Act), will add an estimated $6.2 trillion to America's primary deficit over the next seventy-five years, according to Government Accountability Office projections.[26]

Other predictions are just as bleak. The Peter G. Peterson Foundation calculates that even with the American Taxpayer Relief Act, passed in January 2013 in order to avoid going over the "fiscal cliff," "federal debt will reach a staggering 200 percent of GDP by 2040."[27] Federal spending per American household has grown by 152 percent over the last four and a half decades from $11,900 in 1965 to $30,015 in 2012, with a projected rise to $34,602 in 2022. Total federal spending since 1970 has increased 288 percent, while median household income has only gone up 24.2 percent during the same period.[28]

The Rise of America's Dependency Culture

Fueling this unsustainable debt is America's bloated and rapidly expanding entitlements system, which will be a yoke around the neck of future generations of taxpayers. As Margaret Thatcher warned, a dependency culture is extremely dangerous for a superpower, draining the resources it needs to defend itself and lead on the world stage: "A society which puts a higher value on state hand-outs to its able-bodied citizens than on measures to protect those citizens from internal crime and external threats is one which risks becoming decadent."[29] Most Americans share Thatcher's concerns. According to a Rasmussen poll conducted in March 2013, 64 percent of Americans believe "there are too many Americans dependent on the government for financial aid," compared to just 8 percent who believe "not enough Americans are dependent on this aid." Just 17 percent of Americans "feel the level of dependency is about right."[30] In addition, as Rasmussen polling finds, 80 percent of Americans agree with the statement "Work is the best solution for poverty," with just 9 percent disagreeing.[31]

Federal welfare spending is projected to grow almost 80 percent in the next ten years, at a total cost of $11 trillion.[32] Based on Congressional Research Service data, total welfare spending now amounts to $168 per day for every household in poverty in America. In contrast the median household income of $50,054 (using 2011 figures) translates to just $137.13 per day.[33] A recent study of the March 2011 U.S. Census Bureau Current Population Survey by The Heritage Foundation's Center for Data Analysis revealed that more than two in five Americans now live on government programs.[34] The report's authors found that "the number of people receiving benefits from the federal government in the United States has grown from under 94 million people in 2000 to more than 128 million people in 2011. That means that 41.3 percent of the U.S. population is now on a federal government program." The Heritage report showed that in 2010, "over 70 percent of federal spending went to dependence-creating programs," with the number of Americans enrolled in at least one federal program growing "more than two times faster than has the U.S. population."[35]

The number of Americans on food stamps in 2013 was a record 47.5 million (almost one in six of the population).[36] There are nearly as many Americans dependent on the welfare state as there are people in the whole of England or Spain. And with unemployment stubbornly stuck between 7 and 8 percent, there is little prospect in the near term of a decline in dependency. The growing reliance on welfare is dangerous for American society and the economy. As Thatcher reminded American journalists at the National Press Club in 1995, drawing from her own experience of confronting the welfare system in Britain, a culture of dependency can only lead to deep-seated malaise and societal decline:

> Welfare dependency is bad for families, and bad for the tax-payer. It makes it less necessary and less worth-while to work. The promotion of idleness leads, as it always does, to the growth of vice, irresponsibility, and crime. The bonds which hold society together are weakened. The bill—for single mothers, for delinquency, for vandalism—mounts. In some areas a generation grows up without solid roots or sound role models, without self-esteem or hope. It is extraordinary what damage is sometimes done in the name of compassion. The task of reversing the growth of welfare dependency and repairing the structure of the traditional family is one of the most difficult we in the West face.[37]

President Obama shows little sign, however, of being willing to reverse the rise of the welfare state in the United States. In fact, his policies are actively advancing them. His second inaugural address was a sharp reminder to America and the world of why he is the most liberal president in U.S. history.[38] In his defiant speech on the steps of the Capitol on a cold January day, Mr. Obama made it clear that he was in no mood for compromise or reaching out across the political aisle. He offered no comfort to the nearly sixty million Americans (47 percent of the electorate) who voted against him in the 2012 presidential election.

Instead, Obama's inaugural speech was a love letter to big government calling for "collective action," greater regulation of the free market, and additional federal programs to "harness new ideas and technology to remake our government." In common parlance, all of this translates into yet more government spending and higher taxes. He also ruled out serious entitlement reform, arguing instead for the status quo, "the commitments we make to each other through Medicare and Medicaid and Social Security." The speech gave little encouragement to the entrepreneurs and small businessmen who drive the U.S. economy and who have been targeted with tax increases.

Barack Obama's America increasingly resembles big-government Europe. This should alarm anyone who cares about the prosperity of the American people. If the United States is to suffer Europe's fate, the future of the leader of the free world will be bleak.

America Is Going down the Same Path as Europe

Europe has been a role model for twenty-first-century decline, with a stagnant economy, high unemployment, massive debts, and falling birthrates. While the United States created almost fifty million new jobs between 1970 and 1999, the figure for Europe was just five million.[39] British prime minister David Cameron has pointed out that "Europe's share of world output is projected to fall by almost a third in the next two decades.... If Europe today accounts for just over 7 percent of the world's population, produces around 25 percent of global GDP and has to finance 50 percent of global social spending, then it's obvious that it will have to work very hard to maintain its prosperity and way of life."[40] The Eurozone is expected to remain in recession until at least 2014. Unemployment in the Eurozone is expected to peak at 12.2 percent (nineteen million people),[41] and the rate in Spain has already hit a staggering 26 percent—55 percent in the case of sixteen- to twenty-four-year-olds.[42]

America is going down the same route taken by a multitude of social democratic governments in Europe over the last half century, erecting a vast welfare system, raising taxes, imposing heavy regulations on businesses, and cultivating dependency. The European Union is a role model for the United States under President Obama. Incredibly, nearly half of Democrats in a November 2012 Rasmussen poll, conducted just after the general election, declared a favorable opinion of socialism, a remarkably high figure for the supporters of the ruling party in the United States.[43]

Europe's nightmare could soon be America's. Washington politicians and pundits have been warning for years that the United States could end up like Greece, whose anarchist riots and violent street protests have captivated the attention of the American public. In reality, America is already in Greek territory in terms of its overall indebtedness. As figures provided by the Republican side of the Senate Budget Committee show, U.S. per-person debt is now 35 percent higher than that of Greece. It is also higher than that of Italy, France, and Spain.[44] The United States is also expected to spend 60 percent more per person than Spain over the next five years,[45] with U.S. per-person debt set to increase at a rate seven times faster than that of Italian debt.[46]

OECD figures for 2012 show that America's government debt as a percentage of GDP (109.8 percent) exceeds that of the Eurozone as a whole (100.6 percent), as well as that of France (105.1 percent) and the

United Kingdom (105.3 percent). In Europe, only Greece (181.3 percent), Italy (127 percent), Portugal (125.6 percent), Iceland (124.7 percent), and Ireland (123.2 percent) still exceed the United States in government gross financial liabilities as a percentage of GDP.[47] According to Senate calculations, the United States is expected to add three times more debt than the Eurozone and United Kingdom combined in the five years beginning in 2013—$5.7 trillion as opposed to $1.9 trillion.[48]

These figures are truly shocking, and they demonstrate just how far down the road America has moved toward European-style decline. It is increasingly difficult to differentiate the policies of the Obama administration from those of continental European governments. Daniel Hannan, a British member of the European Parliament and a leading Eurosceptic, has pointed out that Barack Obama shares many ideological traits with his European Union counterparts, which explains why Washington's outlook so resembles Brussels's: "My guess is that if anything, Obama would verbalize his ideology using the same vocabulary that Eurocrats do … in other words, President Obama wants to make the U.S. more like the EU."[49]

Is America Becoming France?

Europe's second biggest economy, France, offers a glimpse of what the United States could become if it continues down the path of higher taxes, class warfare, and the politics of envy. François Hollande's victory in May 2012 was a symbol of the European Union's relentless decline and a firm rejection of the kind of free-market policies that are needed to get countries like France back on their feet. A supporter of the kind of deeply entrenched socialist policies that continue to cripple Europe's economies, Hollande declared that "the world of finance" is his "true enemy."[50] His government's agenda is a symbol of everything that is wrong with Europe today.

The French Socialists' proposed 75-percent marginal income tax rate on anyone earning more than one million euros ($1.3 million) a year provoked an exodus of some of the country's wealthiest citizens, who escaped to lower-tax territories. Among the tax refugees was France's most famous actor, Gérard Depardieu, who relinquished his citizenship and fled to Russia, which has a flat 13-percent tax rate.[51] London opened its doors to another wave of French immigrants who joined the hundreds of thousands of French exiles already living across the Channel. London's upscale borough of Chelsea and Kensington has even been dubbed "the twenty-first *arrondissement*." In October and November 2012 alone, fifty-three billion euros ($69 billion) flowed out of France as dismayed investors anticipated Hollande's "millionaire tax,"[52] and the French economy slid back into recession. Even France's labor minister, Michel Sapin, declared in January 2013 that France is "totally bankrupt."[53] The government's income tax plan was subsequently slapped down by France's Constitutional Council, prompting Hollande to replace it with a new 75-percent tax for companies paying salaries above one million euros.[54]

It is an indictment of U.S. government policy that French politicians are now citing Obama's bailouts of the American automotive industry as their inspiration. When the Socialist government sought to nationalize the Indian-owned steel company ArcelorMittal, the industry minister, Arnaud Montebourg, answered critics, "Barack Obama's nationalized. The Germans are nationalizing. All countries are nationalizing. I've also noticed the British nationalized six banks."[55] It is little wonder that Hollande joked during his campaign, "Obama and I have the same advisers."[56]

Barack Obama's rhetoric is strikingly similar to François Hollande's. They both emphasize making the rich "pay a little more," they both like to attack bankers and corporations, and they talk incessantly about "equality." These policies invariably drive out both wealthy individuals and investment capital.

America Needs Economic Freedom

Both François Hollande and Barack Obama have declared war on economic freedom, the foundation of prosperity. In the 2013 Heritage Foundation–*Wall Street Journal* Index of Economic Freedom,[57] France ranks thirtieth out of forty-three European countries, and its humiliating sixty-third place globally puts it behind Albania, El Salvador, and Mexico. In many ways France is a warning to America, with both countries headed by left-wing presidents committed to expanding the role of the state and raising taxes.

America still ranks much higher in the index than France, but it has been steadily declining for the last few years. The world's largest economy now ranks tenth in the world in economic freedom, behind Denmark, Mauritius, Chile, and Canada. This is the fifth year in a row that U.S. economic freedom has declined. America's corporate tax rate, at 35 percent, is now one of the highest in the Western world.

Economic freedom matters. It is intricately linked with prosperity, economic growth, and wealth creation. As Margaret Thatcher put it in a speech at Georgetown University in 1981, "In the Declaration of Independence we find the principle of economic freedom firmly embedded in the 'pursuit of happiness'. This freedom—the freedom for a man to work for whomever he will, to enter into voluntary agreements and partnerships, to buy and to sell, to save and to invest—this freedom for enterprise is the foundation upon which the unparalleled prosperity of the West is built."[58]

In the same speech, Thatcher proposed four principles that advance economic freedom:

- The "soundness of money," including "fighting inflation and strengthening the dollar as the main prop of the international monetary system";

- The "old lesson of cutting our coat according to our cloth," or reining in public spending;
- Letting markets function freely, with limited state intervention, coupled with free trade internationally; and
- Reducing "the excessive dependence of Western economies on imported oil," which she believed increased inflation and unemployment and reduced growth.

Thatcher always regarded economic freedom, along with representative democracy and the rule of law, as one of the three pillars of modern liberty. In the Winston Churchill Memorial Lecture, delivered in Luxembourg soon after she became prime minister, she affirmed, "Representative political institutions cannot alone guarantee our liberties. It is economic liberty that nourishes the enterprise of those whose hard work and imagination ultimately determine the conditions in which we live."[59]

America's Decline Is Not Inevitable

There is nothing inevitable about American decline. America has much to learn from Margaret Thatcher's refusal to see her country remain as the sick man of Europe. As "decline and surrender were just not good enough for Britain,"[60] so they are not good enough for the United States. Decline, of course, is not measured only by economic data. It is a state of mind that saps a nation's will to lead. If Britain, which suffered profound self-doubt after the loss of its empire by the mid-twentieth century, could regain its pride on the world stage, so can America, with the right conservative leadership in place.

Americans must remember what Margaret Thatcher told an audience of conservative activists in 1982: "We can't avoid one unchallengeable truth. The Government has no money of its own. All that it has it takes in taxes or borrows at interest. It's all of you—everyone here—that pays."[61]

The private sector, not the federal government, generates prosperity. If the United States will not control government spending, it will not remain the world's only superpower. In the absence of American leadership, anti-democratic regimes will grow in strength. As the Obama administration continues its destructive agenda into a second term, the American people are waking up to the danger. A Rasmussen poll in January 2013 revealed that "just 28 percent of likely U.S. voters now prefer a larger government with more services and higher taxes to a smaller one with fewer services and lower taxes."[62]

The Left's attempt to refashion America into a kind of supersized Belgium with Greek-style debt, if successful, will end in economic disaster. Conservatives at every level must fight it with all their strength on every front. There is nothing to be gained by the United States' emulating the European social and economic model.

As Margaret Thatcher reminded the British people when she was prime minister, there is no such thing as "public money," but only the hard-earned money of the taxpayer, which deserves to be spent wisely and in a prudent manner:

> One of the great debates of our time is about how much of your money should be spent by the State and how much you should keep to spend on your family. Let us never forget this fundamental truth: the State has no source of money other than money which people earn themselves. If the State wishes to spend more it can do so only by borrowing your savings or by taxing you more. It is no good thinking that someone else will pay—that "someone else" is you. There is no such thing as public money; there is only taxpayers' money.[63]

Key Leadership Lessons

- Thatcher demonstrated that decline can be reversed. A great leader never concedes that a country's best days are behind it.

- Socialism has not worked in Europe, and it will not work in America either.

- Economic freedom, not big government, is vital to wealth creation and prosperity.

- America can avoid Europe's fate by reining in government spending, reducing the size of the welfare state, cutting down on government regulation, lowering taxes, and advancing fundamental entitlement reform.

- It is in America's interest to support national sovereignty in Europe and a strong transatlantic alliance based on bilateral ties with key U.S. allies.

- America's conservatives must support those in Europe who are fighting for the principles of sovereignty, individual liberty, and economic freedom.

- American decline is not inevitable, but it will take another conservative revolution to reverse it.

CHAPTER SIX

REJECTING APPEASEMENT: LESSONS FROM THE COLD WAR

"Dictators can be deterred, they can be crushed—but they can never be appeased."
—MARGARET THATCHER, SPEECH TO
CONSERVATIVE PARTY CONFERENCE, OCTOBER 12, 1990[1]

Margaret Thatcher's premiership was marked by firm leadership on the world stage, the kind of international statesmanship that has become virtually extinct in the second decade of the twenty-first century. The Russians named her the Iron Lady with good reason—she was resolute in her opposition to the Soviet empire and unyielding in her condemnation of the Communist system. They found her a formidable adversary, and over time, even the enemies of freedom had to concede that her beliefs were indomitable.

Together with Ronald Reagan, Thatcher confronted, defied, and ultimately brought down a totalitarian ideology that had cast a huge shadow of tyranny over much of Europe for nearly half a century. "In the deepest sense," she said, "this victory was that of the human spirit itself against those who sought to subjugate mankind to their own evil ends."[2] The Communist Party, which had ruled the Soviet Union through fear, was, as Thatcher pointed out to students in Krakow, Poland, at the end of the Cold War, "like a monstrous parasite which consumes the flesh of its host and leaves behind a shell."[3] She later reminded the world of the need never to forget the horrors of communism, a fundamentally evil system that cost tens of millions of lives in the twentieth century, in many cases far beyond the borders of Russia:

> We must keep alive the memory of the scale of the threat to us and the depths of the suffering endured by generations in those countries which were enslaved by the Soviet system. We must never forget, or allow future generations to forget. In sheer numbers those who lost their lives as a result of Communism far outstrip even those who died as a result of Nazism—and Communism, despite the fall of the Soviet empire, has not yet been eliminated from the world.[4]

Appeasement, in Thatcher's view, was always a sign of weakness, a betrayal of the national interest, and a message to Britain's enemies that it did not have the stomach for the battle ahead. In an interview, one journalist accused her of holding an "extraordinarily pessimistic worldview" that was incompatible with Thatcher's Christian faith. The prime minister's forthright response epitomized her rejection of appeasement, reminding her countrymen that "Christianity allows self-defense":

> Did you hope that Hitler wouldn't attack Britain? Do you think it would have helped us, just having hope? Do you think it

would have helped the future of Christianity to have it extinguished? Christianity allows self-defence. On your world, we wouldn't be here now. We'd have just sat back and said ... some people are pacifists. I respect them for it. They were very courageous, some people, being pacifists. They went into the front line. They did ... some of the Quakers treated people. They're very, very brave. But what you're saying is a Stalin, a Hitler—just sit back and hope for the best. No, that is not any belief that I know of Christianity.[5]

Thatcher's determination to resist tyrants and to reject the temptation of appeasement was influenced by her admiration, from a young age, of Sir Winston Churchill. "It was the War years," noted Thatcher looking back from the 1990s, "which most affected my wider outlook on events.... The remarkable oratory of Winston Churchill was now indelibly imprinted on my mind. I believed then (and I believe now) that the principle that aggression must not be allowed to pay is fundamental to a just and orderly world."[6]

As a schoolgirl in Grantham during World War II, Thatcher would sit with her family around the radio, listening to Churchill's words of defiance in the face of Hitler's attempts to invade Britain and conquer Europe. Churchill's declaration "I have nothing to offer but blood, toil, tears, and sweat" and his pledge of "victory at all costs—victory in spite of terror" shaped her worldview. To Thatcher, "everything about Churchill was heroic"—he was "a leader, a man among men." As she recalled in a speech at Blenheim Palace near Oxford, Churchill's birthplace, "For me, and so many others, our ideas of liberty, of honour, of sacrifice, of fellowship, of valour—our idea of Britain herself—have been formed by Churchill's words."[7]

Throughout her political career, Thatcher drew strength and inspiration from Churchill's leadership, especially at moments when she faced huge challenges, key moments in history that called for ironclad resolve. She also drew comfort from remembering that Churchill had often found himself alone politically, scorned by many in his own party, but nevertheless determined to stand by his principles.

The Perils of Appeasement

The world is no less dangerous today, perhaps even more so, but Washington and the capitals of Europe display weakness, complacency, and apathy, which embolden the enemies of the free world. Thatcher warned, "There will always be conflict: it is part of human nature, part of the eternal battle between good and evil. There will always be those who are prepared to use force to attain their objectives—dictators will not suddenly become an extinct species."[8]

In many respects the world is even more dangerous than in the era of Thatcher and Reagan. America faces not a single major adversary but an array of dangerous rogue regimes, North Korea and Iran heading the list. While Russia remains a threat in eastern Europe, China is emerging as the superpower of the East, vastly expanding its military capacity while its economic might grows from Africa to Latin America. Even with the killing of Osama bin Laden, al Qaeda remains a threat with its global network of Islamist terrorists, many operating within the free world itself, particularly in western Europe.

Despite the threats, we find ourselves in the second age of Jimmy Carter. An administration befuddled by utopianism sends diplomats scurrying across the globe to engage our enemies while it scales back American defenses and commitments on the world stage. We know how the Carter era ended: with an even more belligerent and emboldened Soviet Union, radical Islamists in control of Iran, a rising Communist threat in Latin America, and a weakened United States.

In his second inaugural address, President Obama called for "peace in our time," urging "the constant advance of those principles that our common creed describes; tolerance and opportunity, human dignity and justice." Obama's poorly chosen words echoed Neville Chamberlain's infamous announcement of "peace for our time" in 1938, just before Europe was torn asunder by the greatest war the world had ever seen.

The Obama administration's foreign policy has been naïve, beginning with a futile videotaped address to "the peoples and leaders of the Islamic Republic of Iran" two months after Obama took office.[9] Adopting a European Union–style policy of "constructive engagement," Washington implemented a softer approach to the Islamist regime in Tehran in the belief that this was a dictatorship that could be negotiated with. Even on the issue of sanctions, the Obama team has been half-hearted, frequently fighting calls from Congress for tougher measures and implementing them only after sustained pressure. By the end of Obama's first term, America faced an emboldened and aggressive Iran, hell-bent on developing nuclear weapons and convinced that the United States lacked the will to use military force against its nuclear facilities.

While treating Iran's ruling Islamists with deference, Obama has failed to show the same consideration for those fighting for freedom in that beleaguered country. When Mahmoud Ahmadinejad claimed victory in Iran's clearly fraudulent presidential election in June 2009, the White House's response was cowardly silence. U.S. officials refused to question the result or even condemn the brutal suppression of protests. Vice President Joe Biden summed up his administration's position in an interview on NBC's *Meet the Press*: "We're going to withhold comment…. I mean we're just waiting to see."[10] While dissidents were spilling their blood in the streets of Tehran, the White House spokesman Robert Gibbs praised "the vigorous debate and enthusiasm this election generated."[11] Even some

European politicians were more vociferous in their condemnation. The German foreign minister summoned the Iranian ambassador to Berlin in protest. At least four hundred demonstrators were killed in the protests following Ahmadinejad's victory.[12] And when huge street protests flared again in December 2009, Obama, vacationing in Hawaii, remained as silent as a Trappist monk.

The unmistakable message from Washington was that the world's superpower was unwilling to speak out against the barbaric suppression of political dissidents by a deeply anti-American regime. Obama's approach to Iran reflects his weakness on the world stage. It is never a good sign when American presidents receive a warm welcome from the United Nations General Assembly, but Obama has made himself a favorite guest with his odes to dreamy liberal idealism.[13] He ranks with Jimmy Carter as the most naïve president in U.S. history.

Obama has extended the hand of friendship to almost every dictatorship on Earth. Zimbabwe, North Korea, and Venezuela can trample on human rights without real censure from an administration that has embraced even the genocidal tyranny in Sudan. Obama's former special envoy to Sudan, retired Air Force Major General J. Scott Gration, explained in 2009, "We've got to think about giving out cookies. Kids, countries—they react to gold stars, smiley faces, handshakes, agreements, talks, engagement."[14]

Obama even transformed the War on Terror into an "Overseas Contingency Operation" while studiously avoiding describing America's enemies as Islamist terrorists.[15] He has gone to great lengths to emphasize that the United States is not engaged in a worldwide war against a vicious Islamist enemy that seeks its destruction. As Joe Biden put it in a speech to the Munich Security Conference in 2009, the United States was involved in "a shared struggle against extremism" and a fight against "a small number of violent extremists [who] are beyond the call of reason."[16] Yet the

September 11, 2012, attack on the U.S. compound in Benghazi and the murder of the American ambassador to Libya demonstrated that al Qaeda remains a serious threat and probably will remain one for decades to come.

The naïveté of the Obama administration was on display most clearly in its celebrated "reset" of American relations with Russia. Seriously misjudging Vladimir Putin—an authoritarian ruler with an extensive KGB background—Obama pursued a policy of full-blown appeasement. It began with what can only be described as a strategic surrender to Moscow in September 2009 with the abandonment of plans for missile defense installations in Poland and the Czech Republic. In a stunning betrayal of these two close and critical allies, Obama humiliated their governments, which had not even been consulted beforehand. Just three months earlier, twenty former ambassadors and heads of state from eastern and central Europe had sent an open letter to Barack Obama urging him not to abandon America's allies in the region. The signatories included many of the great dissidents who had stood up to the Soviet Union, including the former Polish president Lech Walesa and the former Czech president Vaclav Havel.[17]

The Obama administration's about-face, shamelessly implemented on the seventieth anniversary of the Russian invasion of Poland, demonstrated extraordinary weakness in the face of Russian aggression. Moscow had tried to bully and cajole the Poles and the Czechs into rejecting the purely defensive installations. They resisted the Russian threats, only to receive a slap in the face from their faithless American allies.

Worse was to come when Obama signed the New START Treaty in April 2010 and pushed hard for ratification by the lame-duck Senate, which complied in a vote of seventy-one to twenty-six in December. The treaty significantly undermines America's ability to deploy an effective global missile defense system. Despite claims by the treaty's supporters,

Ronald Reagan never would have signed an agreement that encumbered "the pursuit of advanced ballistic missile defense technology."[18]

Toward the end of his compliant first term, Obama promised Moscow even more cooperation once the inconvenient detail of his reelection was out of the way. In a display of astonishing supplication before a major strategic adversary, Obama told then President Dmitry Medvedev in a private conversation (picked up on a microphone and relayed to the world) that he would have "more flexibility" on missile defense after the election, and that it was important "to give me space." Medvedev simply responded by saying: "I understand. I will transmit this information to Vladimir."[19] Moscow's obvious preference for Obama in the election of 2012 was no surprise. "Let me tell you that no one wishes the re-election of Barack Obama as U.S. president as I do," Medvedev told the *Financial Times*.[20] Obama betrayed no embarrassment about the endorsement.

Lessons from the Cold War

Margaret Thatcher and Ronald Reagan pursued the opposite policy during the Cold War. "Resolve," not "reset," was the order of the day. Both leaders understood that adversaries could be effectively countered only through strength, and not weakness.

Today, it is difficult to distinguish the foreign policy of the United States from the foreign policies of most members of the European Union. They share an inordinate deference to the United Nations and supranationalism, an undue faith in engagement with adversaries, and falling defense spending.

It is often presumed, and frequently argued by revisionist historians, that the end of the Soviet empire was the result of internal economic collapse. The resolve of the Western allies, including America's rearmament, was irrelevant to the fall of communism. The revisionists seek to downplay the threat posed by the USSR, and some of them try to obscure the brutal

A young Margaret Roberts with her beloved father, Alfred. © THATCHER FOUNDATION

Working as a research chemist in 1950, the year she first stood for elected office.
© U.S. GOVERNMENT, STATE DEPARTMENT

At her desk in her
parliamentary
office in Finchley,
North London.
© AMY MILNER

With the British Army on the Rhine, at the front line of the Cold War in Europe.
© CROWN, UK GOVERNMENT

Visiting British troops in the Falklands, 1983, the year after they were liberated from Argentina. © CROWN, UK GOVERNMENT

The Iron Lady in commanding form on the world stage, Paris, 1990. FRENCH GOVERNMENT

Speaking at a London dinner for President Reagan, who inscribed the photo to his friend and ally. © U.S. GOVERNMENT, WHITE HOUSE

Dear Margaret — As you c
saying. I a
S

e, I agree with every word you are
do. Warmest Friendship.
Ron

Three great leaders of the twentieth century. Standing alongside Ronald Reagan under the watchful gaze of Sir Winston Churchill, 1984. © U.S. GOVERNMENT

At the helm. Leading an all-male British Cabinet, 1983. © CROWN, UK GOVERNMENT

At ease with Defense Secretary Donald Rumsfeld and Marine Gen. Peter Pace, chairman of the Joint Chiefs of Staff, on a visit to the Pentagon. © U.S. GOVERNMENT, DEPARTMENT OF DEFENSE

With fellow conservatives at a dinner in Washington.
© HERITAGE FOUNDATION

Accepting The Heritage Foundation's Clare Boothe
Luce Award from Vice President Dick Cheney, 2002.
© HERITAGE FOUNDATION

nature of the regime. This view of the fall of the Soviet Union is utterly inaccurate.

Crippled as it was by the contradictions of socialism, the Soviet Union did indeed suffer internal weaknesses. But the peaceful revolution would not have taken place without the steadfast leadership and determination of Ronald Reagan and Margaret Thatcher. Their willingness to stand up to tyranny, both in word and in deed, convinced the Soviets that their cause was unsustainable. The United States and Great Britain won the Cold War because they had leaders who were committed to the freedom of hundreds of millions of people living under tyranny. The free world, led by Reagan and Thatcher, was prepared to confront evil. A decade after the fall of the Soviet Union, Thatcher warned in a speech at the Hoover Institution, "If we learn the wrong lessons from the Cold War, we shall also risk the peace. If we come to believe that the best way to avoid danger is to evade rather than confront it; if we think that negotiation is always the statesmanlike option; if we prefer empty multilateral gestures to powerful national responses, then we shall pay a heavy price—and our children, and grandchildren, will pay it too."[21]

Thatcher described the end of the Cold War as "the most important event in my political life."[22] From a very early age she learned about the evils of communism and was "transfixed and horrified" by accounts of Stalin's terror that had filtered through to the West. The more she read about communism, the more she hated it.[23] It was her Christian upbringing that shaped her views of the rising Soviet menace. In a speech in Moscow after the Cold War, she recalled,

> Brought up in a Christian family, nurtured in liberty, believing in the sanctity and dignity of the individual, and that each of us is responsible for his own actions—how could it be, I thought, that a few Communists under the pretence of freedom

for all men had seized power for themselves, only to extinguish the freedom of all others. The people over whom they ruled so brutally, were composed of men and women, who were their equals in human rights, in intelligence and who had been born with the ability to plan, think and judge for themselves. They were made of the same flesh and blood as the new despots. This was the new tyranny of the century into which I was born.[24]

Her views on communism were also shaped by Churchill, who had famously declared in the House of Commons in 1919, "Bolshevism is not a policy: it is a disease."[25] As leader of the Opposition and then as prime minister, Thatcher realized that "this great contest was between the Western system conforming to the needs and habits of ordinary human beings, freely cooperating in markets, and Communism, in which a false ideology directed every aspect of social and economic life towards self-destructive ends."[26]

Three decades after Churchill's "Iron Curtain" speech in Fulton, Missouri, Margaret Thatcher issued a warning to the West that "the Russians are bent on world dominance." In her "Iron Lady" speech of January 1976, she declared:

If we cannot understand why the Russians are rapidly becoming the greatest naval and military power the world has ever seen, if we cannot draw the lesson of what they tried to do in Portugal and are now trying to do in Angola, then we are destined—in their words—to end up on "the scrap heap of history"....

There are moments in our history when we have to make a fundamental choice. This is one such moment—a moment when our choice will determine the life or death of our kind of society—and the future of our children. Let's ensure that our children will have cause to rejoice that we did not forsake their freedom.[27]

Thatcher's Soviet strategy rested on six principles. First, the enemy had to be seen for what it was—a deadly threat. Second, the West must rebuild its military might to deter Soviet aggression, with NATO as the cornerstone of transatlantic defense. Third, the free world should support dissidents behind the Iron Curtain. Fourth, the West must demonstrate to the Russian people the moral contrast between freedom and communism. Fifth, the West should work with reformers in the USSR to encourage change from within. Sixth, and perhaps most important of all, Great Britain and the United States must be united in leading the West in confronting and defeating the Soviet empire. Further consideration of these principles shows that they are no less important today than they were during the Cold War.

1. Identify the Enemy

Margaret Thatcher was not shy about stating exactly what the Soviet Union was—a ruthless tyranny intent on global domination and the subjugation of the West. Communism itself "was only the extreme form of the socialist plague."[28] These are important lessons for today, as the West faces a growing threat from Islamist terrorism and its state sponsors. The first step toward defeating a tyrannical adversary is to identify exactly what you are fighting and what your opponent stands for.

Robin Harris, a senior advisor to Thatcher for several decades, recently discussed a related principle that she followed:

When Margaret Thatcher negotiated with Communists about human rights, she had a self-imposed rule. It was to deliver the same message in private as in public. That was, and is, unusual.

Politicians prefer bold and indignant speeches at home to bruising confrontations with foreign leaders face to face. But you have to do it. The reason is simple. It is because, whatever someone's ideology, he will not take you seriously as a human being if he thinks you don't really care about the causes you espouse. When the Soviet leaders understood that Ronald Reagan and Mrs. Thatcher were deadly serious about the rights of people who, in Soviet eyes, didn't really matter at all, the Kremlin also grasped that Western leaders were serious about wider strategy—Afghanistan, subversion, weaponry and the rest.[29]

2. Rebuild the West's Military Capability

Margaret Thatcher was determined "to make it clear to the Communists that they would never win by military might."[30] She argued that the first duty of government is to "safeguard its people against external aggression. To guarantee the survival of our way of life."[31] That was not, however, the view of her socialist predecessors in government, who shamefully ran down Britain's defenses in the 1970s. The United Kingdom spent less per capita on defense in 1976 than many of its NATO allies, and further cuts were planned.[32] Three years before she entered Downing Street, British spending per capita was substantially lower than that of West Germany, France, and even neutral Sweden. This neglect, Thatcher noted, was "the disastrous economic legacy of Socialism." The United States spent more than twice as much per capita as the United Kingdom did.[33]

Yet the Russians were outdoing even the Americans in military investment. Thatcher pointed out in the "Iron Lady" speech that the Russians were "spending 20 percent more each year than the United States on military research and development, 25 percent more on weapons and equipment, [and] 60 percent more on strategic nuclear forces." In the preceding decade, Russia had "spent 50 percent more than the United States on naval shipbuilding." Moscow had quadrupled its number of nuclear submarines over the same period, constructing a new one every month.[34] In central Europe, the Warsaw Pact outnumbered NATO by 150,000 troops, ten thousand tanks, and 2,600 aircraft.[35] By 1976, Russia was spending a staggering 11 to 12 percent of its gross national product on defense (a growth rate of 4 percent a year in real terms), compared with 6.7 percent for the United States and a NATO average of 4.5 percent.[36] By the 1980s, the Soviet figure had risen to between 12 and 14 percent of GNP (five times the officially published figures), rising as high as 25 to 30 percent by 1989.[37] In 1980 alone, the Soviets built 1,600 combat aircraft, three thousand tanks, and 1,500 intercontinental intermediate range missiles.[38]

When she came to office in 1979, Margaret Thatcher was determined to reverse the decline in British defense spending. British defense spending rose by over 20 percent between 1980 and 1985.[39] By 1983, Britain was spending 5.1 percent of GNP on defense, compared with an average of 3.5 percent across the NATO alliance.[40] She firmly rejected the Labour Party's calls for a non-nuclear defense policy and insisted that there be an independent British nuclear deterrent. Thatcher dismissed the idea of a nuclear-free world as "pie in the sky,"[41] "an infantile fantasy."[42] She was convinced that nuclear weapons made the world more secure and war less likely, and Britain, in 1983, became the first country in Europe to station American nuclear cruise missiles on its soil. The Labour leader, Neil Kinnock, defended his party's rejection of nuclear weapons in the face of the Soviet threat, including the removal of all American nuclear bases in the country, by saying that if the Russians invaded, "you've got to make the occupation totally untenable." As Thatcher quipped in response, "Labour's non-nuclear defence policy is a policy for defeat, surrender, occupation, and finally, prolonged guerilla fighting."[43]

Rearming Britain was at the heart of Thatcher's agenda, and she made it a central plank in her 1987 campaign, which saw her reelected for a third term as prime minister. As she told a Conservative rally in Solihull, in the heart of Britain's industrial Midlands, "If Britain were to abandon its defence of liberty, we wouldn't just decline comfortably into a Swedish neutrality. It would be the abandonment of belief in ourselves, a cracking of the cornerstone of the Atlantic Alliance. It really is that serious."[44]

3. Stand with Dissidents

Margaret Thatcher believed that the free world must support those bravely fighting for liberty in the Soviet Union. She told a gathering of British Conservatives in 1975:

> When the Soviet leaders jail a writer, or a priest, or a doctor or a worker, for the crime of speaking freely, it is not only for humanitarian reasons that we should be concerned. For these acts reveal a regime that is afraid of truth and liberty; it dare not allow its people to enjoy the freedoms we take for granted, and a nation that denies those freedoms to its own people will have few scruples in denying them to others. If détente is to progress then it ought to mean that the Soviet authorities relax their ruthless opposition to all forms and expressions of dissent.[45]

She frequently quoted Aleksandr Solzhenitsyn, who had been exiled from Russia in 1974, and who had warned against "the weakness of the West" in the face of Soviet aggression.[46] "Solzhenitsyn could not be ignored," said Thatcher in a speech in Brussels in 1978, "nor could his quiet disappearance be arranged. In some ways the pen is still mightier than the sword."[47] Thatcher was the most prominent leader in Europe holding the Communist regime to account over its abuse of human rights and spoke out regularly against Moscow's violation of the 1975 Helsinki Accords. Soon after the accords were signed, she condemned the KGB's suppression of a group of nine human rights activists led by the nuclear physicist Yuri Orlov, shining an international spotlight on their plight. Addressing a Conservative rally in 1976, she spoke against "the persecution of intellectual dissidents, and of religious minorities—Jews and Baptists in particular," telling her audience that to the Soviets "freedom of information consists of their absolute right to tell their subjects what they should believe and what they should hear." She quoted Yelena Bonner, the wife of Andrei Sakharov, who just weeks earlier had said that "our life is proceeding in such a way that you can't even call it life in the human sense of the word."[48]

As prime minister, Thatcher made a point of meeting with as many dissidents from Russia or Eastern Europe as she could,[49] assuring Moscow that Britain would not turn a blind eye to their plight. "Their fate," she said, "should remind us every day not to take our freedom, our justice, for granted, but to resolve to defend them."[50] Thatcher also insisted on holding talks with dissidents—including Andrei Sakharov and a group of Jewish refuseniks led by Josif Begun—on her historic official visit to Moscow in 1987. She was an outspoken proponent of their cause while many in the West chose to ignore their suffering or were unwilling to stand up to the Russians. In an interview with the London *Sunday Times* at the end of the Cold War, Thatcher praised the courage of the people who had stood up to the might of the Soviet machine, often at great personal cost and with tremendous personal dignity:

> The people who have achieved most in terms of political change in my generation have been the dissidents and refusniks in the Soviet Union and in Eastern Europe—the Sakharovs, the Shcharanskys, the Amoriks, the Bukovskys—and they

took a decision right at the beginning, they would never resort to violence, the Orlovs, all of them, there are so many of them and thousands whose names we do not know, they would never resort to violence, never. And look what they have achieved.[51]

4. Win the Ideological War

"The Cold War," Margaret Thatcher argued, "was a struggle between two sharply opposing systems, encapsulating two wholly contradictory philosophies, involving two totally different objectives."[52] To the Iron Lady, the Cold War represented "the total triumph of our fundamental political beliefs of freedom and justice and democracy, the total triumph. I wonder why we ever doubted it. I wonder why at one time our theory was to constrain the advance of communism, not to defeat it."[53] She explained the West's victory: "An empire has crashed—but not just an empire of armies, slaves and tyrants. The empire was also one of ideas and dogmas. And when those failed, an empire of lies and propaganda. It fell because it was resolutely opposed. Opposed not simply by an alliance of free peoples—though certainly by that—but by the ideas of liberty, free enterprise, private property and democracy."[54]

Thatcher enthusiastically accepted the challenge set by Yuri Andropov in June 1983 when he spoke of an "ideological struggle" for "the minds and hearts of billions of people on the planet."[55] She took every opportunity to advance this message of freedom in Soviet-occupied Europe. She believed that it was the responsibility of the free world "to keep the lamps of freedom burning bright, so that all who look to the West from the shadows of the East, need never doubt that we remain true to those human and spiritual values that lie at the heart of human civilization."[56]

She made her first visit to a Warsaw Pact country, Hungary, in 1984, where she received a distinctly warm welcome from shoppers in Budapest's central market.[57] It was the first of many forays she would make behind the Iron Curtain in the final years of the Cold War, where she would deliver a message of liberty and hope to tens of millions yearning for freedom. It was the same message she brought to Moscow in 1987 when she first met with Mikhail Gorbachev on Soviet soil. It was a trip she later described as "the most important foreign visit I had made."[58] While in Russia, she was unstinting in her calls for greater respect for human rights, and she pressed for the release of prisoners of conscience. Interviewed on Soviet television, she made a point of robustly defending the fundamental freedoms enjoyed in the West: "Freedom of speech, freedom of worship, freedom from fear, and freedom from want; a much more open society means that you discuss all of the things in the same way as we do."[59]

On that same trip to Russia, Thatcher visited the newly reopened Russian Orthodox monastery at Zagorsk, outside Moscow, in a demonstration of solidarity with that country's Christians, who had for decades been forced to worship in private by the Communist authorities. She hosted Russian refuseniks who had suffered heavy persecution by the state at the British embassy. On a walkabout in a grim suburban Moscow housing estate, Thatcher was greeted by a huge, cheering crowd, clearly enamored with her message of liberty.[60] It was a remarkable moment—throngs of Muscovites applauding the Iron Lady amid the bitter cold.

Large crowds also greeted Thatcher on her visit to Poland in 1988. When she arrived at the Gdansk shipyard, "every inch of it seemed taken up with shipyard workers waving and cheering." She met with the Solidarity leader, Lech Walesa, and visited the Church of St. Brygida, packed with worshippers who sang the Solidarity anthem, "God give us back our free Poland." Her message to General Wojciech Jaruzelski, the last Communist ruler of Poland, was firm and unyielding—Solidarity could not be ignored.[61] Just two years later, Walesa was Poland's president, and Communist rule had become history.

Fittingly, in the dying days of the USSR in 1991, the Iron Lady was invited to address the Supreme Soviet. Her speech was a tribute to the triumph of freedom in the face of tyranny, a reminder to her hosts that the ideals of liberty cannot be crushed by totalitarianism: "History tells us of Man's striving to be free. You may use brute force to crush a nation: but you cannot destroy its identity and pride. You can forbid individuals to employ their talents to better their families: but in the end some will be more equal than others. You can fight a war against truth by every means at your disposal: but ultimately truth will win the battle of ideas."[62]

5. Work with Reformers

Margaret Thatcher was the first Western leader to identify Mikhail Gorbachev as a figure within the Soviet system who could bring about change. She was "convinced that we must seek out the most likely person in the rising generation of Soviet leaders and then cultivate and sustain him, while recognizing the clear limits of our power to do so."[63] She described Gorbachev as "a person of great vision and boldness and courage."[64] Thatcher hosted Gorbachev and his wife, Raisa, at Chequers in December 1984, during the Gorbachevs' first visit to a capitalist country in Europe. In her meeting with Gorbachev, just prior to his taking over as general secretary of the Communist Party, she called on the Soviet authorities to allow ordinary people, especially Jews, to leave Russia easily. She also informed Gorbachev that she supported Reagan's plans for a missile defense system, telling him there would be no question of a division between the United States and Great Britain on this matter.[65] She concluded by telling the world's media that she was "cautiously optimistic," and that "we can do business together."[66]

Ultimately, Gorbachev's economic and political reforms, known as *perestroika* ("restructuring") and *glasnost* ("openness"), weakened the grip of Communist rule in Russia. In 1989, she credited Gorbachev with playing a pivotal role in the fall of the Berlin Wall, declaring in front of 10 Downing Street that "none of this would have happened without the vision and courage of Mr. Gorbachev."[67] Thatcher's role in introducing Gorbachev to the West, and at times acting as an intermediary between him and Reagan, proved vital. Through his meetings with Thatcher and with Reagan, Gorbachev saw the unbreakable resolve of the West. Thatcher pressed Gorbachev to increase the freedom of the Russian people. As she put it in her March 1987 speech to the Conservative Central Council just ahead of her first official visit to the Soviet Union,

> When I go to Moscow to meet Mr. Gorbachev next week, my goal will be a peace based not on illusion or surrender, but on realism and strength. But, you can't have peace by a declaration of intent. Peace needs confidence and trust between countries and peoples. Peace means an end to the killing in Cambodia, an end to the slaughter in Afghanistan.
>
> It means honouring the obligations which the Soviet Union freely accepted in the Helsinki Final Act in 1975 to allow free movement of people and ideas and other basic human rights…. We shall reach our judgments not on words, not on intentions, not on promises; but on actions and on results.[68]

6. America and Britain Must Lead

Without the leadership of the United States and Great Britain, the Soviet empire would not have collapsed with the speed and in the manner in which it did. In Thatcher's view, Ronald Reagan rightly "deserves to be regarded as the supreme architect of the Cold War's victory." As Thatcher pointed out, Reagan's plans for the Strategic Defense Initiative (SDI), known as "Star Wars" to its detractors, were decisive. The Soviets, with their ailing economy and limited technology, could not match the deployment of the SDI, the "single most important" decision of Reagan's presidency.[69] As she wrote in *Statecraft*, "It was the American President who had effectively just won the Cold War—without firing a shot.... Mr. Gorbachev had crossed his Rubicon. The Soviets had been forced to accept that the strategy they had pursued since the 1960s—of using weaponry, subversion and propaganda to make up for their internal weakness and so retain superpower status—had finally and definitively failed."[70]

But Thatcher's support of the American superpower was essential to victory. "Without Britain's wholehearted support for the Reagan administration," Thatcher later recalled, "I am not sure that it would have been able to carry its allies along the right path. I also think that the fact that Ronald Reagan and I spoke the same language (in every sense) helped convince friend and foe alike that we were serious."[71] And in the words of President George H. W. Bush, whose administration witnessed the final demise of Communist rule in Europe, "Her resolution and dedication set an example for all of us. She showed that you can't lock people behind walls forever when moral conviction uplifts their souls. And she knew tyranny is powerless against the primacy of the heart. Margaret Thatcher helped bring the Cold War to an end, helped the human will outlast bayonets and barbed wire."[72]

Margaret Thatcher, Freedom Fighter

Today, tens of millions of people in eastern and central Europe owe their freedom to the Iron Lady. As Margaret Thatcher reminded an audience of British Conservatives in 1990 at the dawn of a new, post-Communist era: "No force of arms, no walls, no barbed wire can for ever suppress the longing of the human heart for liberty and independence. Their courage found allies. Their victory came about because for forty long, cold years the West stood firm against the military threat from the

East. Free enterprise overwhelmed Socialism. This government stood firm against all those voices raised at home in favour of appeasement."[73]

The lessons for American conservatives today are clear. Effective international leadership requires a willingness to fight for the cause of freedom. It requires the ability to project power, to deter adversaries, and to defeat them when necessary. "Peace," said Churchill, "will not be preserved by pious sentiments."[74] It can be achieved only with a strong national defense. Liberty can be costly. Freedom, said Margaret Thatcher in New York, is "the great gift of Western culture to mankind," a legacy that must be protected from those who seek to destroy it:

> Freedom is the most contagious of ideas and the one most destructive of tyranny. That is why tyrants of every kind have fought—still fight—so hard to destroy it. They will always fail because where freedom is the heritage of centuries, as in your country and mine, it is tenaciously defended. and because where it is newly established, it inspires confidence and hope. Nowhere and never has it been consciously surrendered....[75]

Key Leadership Lessons

- A powerful leader never bows to evil, but always confronts it, a principle that both Thatcher and Reagan put into practice.
- Appeasement of your enemies is a policy of weakness and defeat. It only emboldens your adversaries.
- Clearly identify the nature of your enemy and what it stands for. There is nothing to be gained by denying reality when facing a dangerous adversary.

- In standing up for human rights, always deliver the same message in private that you do in public.
- Always stand firmly on the side of freedom in the face of totalitarian regimes. Give hope to those who are risking their lives for liberty.
- Make your voice heard in support of political dissidents fighting against tyranny, and demonstrate that you are with them in words and actions.

CHAPTER SEVEN

THE LEADERSHIP LESSONS OF THE FALKLANDS WAR

"We have ceased to be a nation in retreat. . . . Britain found herself again in the South Atlantic and will not look back from the victory she has won."
— MARGARET THATCHER, SPEECH TO CONSERVATIVE PARTY RALLY, CHELTENHAM, JULY 3, 1982[1]

The Falklands War of 1982 was a defining moment in modern British history. The victory revived a sense of national greatness in Britain after decades of decline. As Thatcher proclaimed at the end of the war, "We have ceased to be a nation in retreat. We have instead a new-found confidence—born in the economic battles at home and tested and found true 8,000 miles away. That confidence comes from the re-discovery of ourselves, and grows with the recovery of our self-respect."[2]

The Falklands victory was an extraordinary feat of leadership—the kind that is sorely lacking in the modern era, on both sides of the Atlantic. The adversaries who underestimated Margaret Thatcher—especially the Argentine military junta that launched the invasion—found them-selves humiliated by a British prime minister who would later write: "When you are at war you cannot allow the difficulties to dominate your thinking: you have to set out with an iron will to overcome them. And anyway what was the alternative? That a common or garden dictator should rule over the Queen's subjects and prevail by fraud and violence? Not while I was Prime Minister."[3]

The war demonstrated the importance of standing up to aggressors and warned the world's dictators that the resolve of free nations was far from extinguished. "We were defending our honour as a nation," said Thatcher, "and principles of fundamental importance to the whole world—above all, that aggressors should never succeed."[4]

Courage and Conviction:
The Liberation of the Falklands

The Falklands War was one of the most brilliantly executed and suc-cessful military campaigns of modern times and a display of extraordinary courage and sacrifice by British forces. It was, as Margaret Thatcher herself described it, "a triumph of endeavour and skill of planning and imagina-tion."[5] The Falkland Islands today remain a British overseas territory. Their three thousand inhabitants elect their own government and enjoy full self-determination. This freedom is due in large part to the unflinch-ing determination of Margaret Thatcher.

The Falkland Islands are an archipelago in the South Atlantic, about 1,200 miles from the capital of Argentina and three hundred miles from the coast of South America. They lie at the entrance to the Antarctic, and their harbors would give them strategic value should the Panama Canal ever be closed. British sailors first landed on the islands in 1690, British sovereignty was established in 1765, and a permanent British settlement was in place by 1833.[6] Even though the overwhelming majority of the inhabitants are of British descent, the Argentine junta, led by General Leopoldo Galtieri, carried out a surprise invasion on Friday, April 2, 1982, and held 1,800 Falkland Islanders captive. Within forty-eight hours, Thatcher's government launched a naval task force to retake the islands, which are more than eight thousand miles from Great Britain.

By Monday the first wave of the task force, led by two aircraft carriers, HMS *Invincible* and HMS *Hermes*, had set sail for the South Atlantic.[7] The islands were liberated eleven weeks later, on June 14, 1982. At its height, the task force included over a hundred ships, three submarines, and twenty-seven thousand sailors, marines, soldiers, and airmen.[8] Launching the task force in such a short period was an extraordinary accomplishment, which demonstrated decisiveness and vision that had been largely absent in British politics since the end of the Churchill era.

Thatcher told the BBC that there was no question in her mind about the right course: "One didn't hesitate for long. Of course one went to the Cabinet with a very, very firm recommendation. There was no hesitation, a total unanimity. We just had to go."[9] In doing so, she defied the views of her own Ministry of Defence, which warned that the islands could not be retaken. As she later recalled, "This was terrible, and totally unacceptable. I could not believe it: these were our people, our islands. I said instantly: 'If they are invaded, we have got to get them back.'" Fortunately, the prime minister was backed by the chief of the Naval Staff, Sir Henry Leach, who did not share the fears of the defense secretary, Sir John Nott. Leach pledged to assemble a task force within two days.[10]

It is not hard to see why the defense chiefs were nervous. This was to be the biggest British military operation since the Suez debacle of 1956, which had ended in humiliation. The last quarter century had been marked by Britain's gradual retreat as a global power. There had been damaging defense cuts in the 1970s, which were only then being reversed. The military operation, coming at a time when rising unemployment was eroding Thatcher's popularity, was politically risky. Britain's armed forces had not been tested on this scale for nearly thirty years, and the British people were still suffering from a debilitating post-imperial lack of confidence. After many years of socialist rule and decades of welfare statism, this did not look like the bulldog warrior nation of World War II or the country that had fought with great courage alongside U.S. forces in the Korean War.

Many of Thatcher's own backbenchers doubted the wisdom of fighting a campaign on the other side of the world. Her recently released personal papers from 1982 reveal considerable opposition to military action in the Falklands. Soon after the Argentine invasion, the government chief whip, Michael Jopling, wrote a memorandum to the new foreign secretary, Francis Pym, delivering a frank assessment of where various members of the Conservative Party stood on the issue of war against Argentina. While some Tory Members of Parliament declared that their "constituents want blood," others urged caution or even expressed outright opposition to war, with calls from some quarters for negotiations with Buenos Aires.

According to Jopling, several MPs took the view that "we must try and get away without a fight," with one begging, "Please no blood." A prominent member of Parliament and historian, Robert Rhodes James, was described by the chief whip as "hopelessly defeatist, depressed and disloyal," while another was "worried that expectations are too high. He feels that the military difficulties may be insurmountable." Ian Gilmour, MP for Chesham and Amersham, was of the view that "we are making a big mistake. It will make Suez look like common sense." Kenneth Clarke, a future cabinet minister under Thatcher, hoped that "nobody thinks we are going to fight the Argentinians. We should blow up a few ships but nothing more." Christopher Patten, who later in the decade became the last governor of Hong Kong, was clearly hedging his bets, offering to "write a supportive article in the press once the situation is clearer." Some MPs were even in favor of striking a deal with Argentina. One even suggested that Britain ought to "let the Argentinians have the Falklands with as little fuss as possible."[11]

While many in her own party went wobbly, the Iron Lady never considered capitulation. She was immovably opposed to any agreement with Argentina short of its complete withdrawal from the Falklands and the preservation of the islanders' right to self-determination. In her announcement to the House of Commons of the launch of the naval task force, she said:

> I must tell the House that the Falkland Islands and their dependencies remain British territory. No aggression and no invasion can alter that simple fact. It is the Government's objective to see that the islands are freed from occupation and are returned to British administration at the earliest possible moment....
>
> The people of the Falkland Islands, like the people of the United Kingdom, are an island race. Their way of life is British; their allegiance is to the Crown. They are few in number, but they have the right to live in peace, to choose their own way of life and to determine their own allegiance.... It is the wish of the British people and the duty of Her Majesty's Government to do everything that we can to uphold that right. That will be our hope and our endeavour and, I believe, the resolve of every Member of the House.[12]

Unlike some of her colleagues in Parliament, on both sides of the political aisle, Margaret Thatcher had faith in Britain's armed forces and in the British character. She refused to believe that Britain was not up to the task and held on to the ideal of the great warrior nation, one that had secured countless victories on battlefields across the world for many centuries. At a salute to the Falklands task force four months after the end of the war, Thatcher quoted the nineteenth-century Anglican cleric Sydney Smith: "I have boundless confidence in the British character.... I believe more heroes will spring up in the hour of danger than all the military nations of ancient and modern Europe have ever produced." She told her audience, "We, the British people, are proud of what has been done, proud of these heroic pages in our island story."[13]

Ultimately, Thatcher went to war out of patriotism. She could not stand to see her countrymen held hostage by a foreign power and British territory seized. She did not accept that an aggressor should get away with brute force and believed that a policy of appeasement was nothing short of surrender. Though many at home and abroad doubted Britain's ability to retake the Falklands, Thatcher cast fear and caution aside and proved that Britain was not a helpless, once-great power.

Against huge odds, the task force recaptured the Falklands seventy-four days after the invasion, capturing fifteen thousand Argentine military personnel. Britain lost 255 servicemen (as well as three Falkland Islanders), and 777 were wounded. Several British ships were sunk by Argentine aircraft using French-made Exocet missiles, including four destroyers and frigates. Argentine casualties amounted to 649 killed and over 1,000 wounded.[14]

The bravery of the British soldiers, sailors, marines, and airmen was extraordinary. Two Victoria Crosses (Britain's highest military honor) were awarded to members of the Parachute Regiment for their roles in the crucial battles of Goose Greene and Mount Longdon. On the twenty-fifth anniversary of the liberation of the Falklands in 2007, Thatcher paid tribute to their heroism, declaring that "no finer troops could be found in the world than those of our country.... Britain's armed services are unmatched in their skill and professionalism. More than that, they are the model of all that we wish our country and citizens to be. The service they offer and the sacrifice they make are an inspiration."[15]

The operation suffered serious setbacks that would have tested the resolve of any leader. The sinking of HMS *Sheffield* early in the war took the lives of twenty sailors and demonstrated the vulnerability of warships to aerial attack. HMS *Coventry* and HMS *Ardent* were sunk in the following weeks, and an Exocet strike on the *Atlantic Conveyor*, a container ship packed with vital supplies, destroyed nearly twenty helicopters.[16] The enemy bombed the landing ships *Sir Tristram* and *Sir Galahad* ahead of the final assault on the Falklands capital, Port Stanley, killing more than thirty Welsh Guards.

Five years later Thatcher recalled, "These were days we will never forget. Anxious nights. The most intensely lived days I can ever remember."[17] Thatcher drew inspiration from the wartime leadership of Sir Winston Churchill. In a 1999 speech at Blenheim Palace, she revealed how the Falklands War had given her "a little insight into the terrible strain faced by Winston Churchill as war-leader when Britain stood alone and at bay, in defence of freedom and civilization."[18]

A Decisive Move:
The Sinking of the *Belgrano*

The sinking of the Argentine cruiser *General Belgrano* on May 2, 1982, was a pivotal moment early in the conflict, prompting the Argentine navy, including its only carrier, to return to port for the duration of the war. The *Belgrano* was reportedly sailing away from the Falklands when it was torpedoed by a British submarine, taking 321 Argentine sailors down with it. The attack proved controversial. Three years later, journalist David Frost questioned Thatcher about the decision, suggesting that the facts about the strike had been covered up. The prime minister shot back, "Do you think, Mr. Frost, that I spend my days prowling round the pigeon holes of the Ministry of Defence to look at the chart of each and every ship? If you do you must be bonkers!" She reminded her critics that the "ship was a danger to our boys. That is why that ship was sunk.... Just because a ship is going in a certain direction does not mean it is sailing away from the field of battle." She ended the interview on a defiant note: "I know it was right to sink her and I would do the same again.... I hope that everyone knows that so long as I am there they have a Prime Minister who will protect our navy, our boys and I will continue to do so."[19]

Thatcher had understood that victory in the Falklands required cutting Argentina's navy off at its knees. The sinking of the *Belgrano* weakened the resolve of the junta and almost certainly accelerated the end of the war, saving many British lives. This was leadership at its best, and Thatcher had nothing to apologize for. Conservative politicians should consult her answer to David Frost when they face hostile questioning from liberal journalists.

The Limits of Diplomacy

Throughout the Falklands conflict, Britain came under intense pressure at the United Nations to negotiate a settlement with Buenos Aires. Additional pressure came from the U.S. State Department and an array of European and Latin American governments. "I was under an almost intolerable pressure to negotiate for the sake of negotiation," Thatcher recalled. "At such a time almost everything and everyone seems to combine to deflect you from what you know has to be done."[20] She insisted, however, that only the complete withdrawal of Argentine forces from the islands and the restoration of British sovereignty would end the hostilities.

Margaret Thatcher always understood that diplomacy was a powerful tool in certain circumstances, especially when backed up by the threat of military force, as the West's resolve in the Cold War amply demonstrated.

But she would never allow it to stand in the way of securing freedom and defending sovereignty, a point she made clear to allies who urged compromise rather than war. Britain did succeed in securing UN Security Council Resolution 502, which demanded the unconditional withdrawal of Argentine forces from the Falklands, based on Article 51 of the Charter of the United Nations—the right to self-defense. But Thatcher "had no illusions as to who would be left to remove the aggressor when all the talking was done: it would be us."[21]

Surprisingly, some of the strongest backing for Thatcher's steadfast position came from French president François Mitterrand, a figure whom she would clash with over Europe in later years. The French backed the British at the UN, as did the Germans. Mitterrand held up a contract to supply Exocet missiles to Peru,[22] an ally of Argentina, preventing more weapons from ending up in the hands of the military junta and probably saving more British warships. Other European countries, however, offered little or no support, and some were more or less hostile, including Spain, Italy, and Ireland. In contrast, the Anglosphere nations of Canada, Australia, and New Zealand were robust in their backing for Britain.

The Reagan administration's role in the Falklands War is often misrepresented and poorly understood. It is true that Washington viewed Argentina as a useful ally against communism in the Americas and was concerned about the potential humiliation of Galtieri's regime. Secretary of State Alexander Haig made numerous attempts to broker an agreement that would avoid a crushing defeat for Argentina. Not for the first time, however, there were important differences of opinion between the State Department and the Pentagon. While U.S. diplomats were publicly urging the avoidance of war, the Reagan administration was quietly providing invaluable military and logistical help to the British. As Thatcher noted, without the Sidewinder air-to-air missiles that the United States supplied, "we could not have retaken the Falklands." America's defense secretary,

Caspar Weinberger, was a staunch supporter of Britain's military effort and had even offered the aircraft carrier *Eisenhower* as "a mobile runway" for British aircraft in the South Atlantic.[23] Thatcher remembered these gestures gratefully: "America never had a wiser patriot, nor Britain a truer friend," than Weinberger.[24]

In an interview during the Versailles Economic Summit Conference, at the height of the Falklands War, President Reagan made it clear whose side he was on when he told a group of Western European TV correspondents that Britain was right to stand up to "a threat that all of us must oppose, and that is the idea that armed aggression can succeed in the world today."[25] He reiterated the point eight days later after meeting with Thatcher in London: "We leave strengthened with the knowledge that the great friendship, the great alliance that has existed for so long between our two peoples, the United Kingdom and the United States, remains and is, if anything, stronger than it has ever been."[26]

The Restoration of British Pride

Margaret Thatcher always knew what she was fighting for. "We fought to show that aggression does not pay and that the robber cannot be allowed to get away with his swag,"[27] and she accomplished that. The British victory also put Moscow on notice that it should not underestimate British resolve. As Thatcher recalled in her autobiography, "The war also had real importance in relations between East and West: years later I was told by a Russian general that the Soviets had been firmly convinced that we would not fight for the Falklands, and that if we did fight we would lose. We proved them wrong on both counts, and they did not forget the fact."[28]

Above all, the Falklands War restored pride in a country that had been steadily retreating from the world since 1945, whose self-confidence had been shattered by the economic decline of the 1970s and the dissolution of a great empire. Margaret Thatcher called it "the Falklands factor," a remarkable revival in the spirit of a nation whose critics, at home and abroad, had written it off as the land of the sinking sun. At the end of the fighting, she declared to a crowd of jubilant supporters:

> When we started out, there were the waverers and the faint-hearts. The people who thought that Britain could no longer seize the initiative for herself. The people who thought we could no longer do the great things which we once did. Those who believed that our decline was irreversible—that we could never again be what we were. There were those who would not admit it—even perhaps some here today—people who would have strenuously denied the suggestion but—in their heart of hearts—they too had their secret fears that it was true: that Britain was no longer the nation that had built an Empire and ruled a quarter of the world.
>
> Well they were wrong. The lesson of the Falklands is that Britain has not changed and that this nation still has those sterling qualities which shine through our history.
>
> This generation can match their fathers and grandfathers in ability, in courage, and in resolution. We have not changed. When the demands of war and the dangers to our own people call us to arms—then we British are as we have always been: competent, courageous and resolute.[29]

Key Leadership Lessons

- Thatcher demonstrated how a strong leader must be prepared to act swiftly and decisively, especially at times of crisis. Procrastination is the antithesis of effective leadership.

- Seek counsel from advisors and colleagues but always be prepared to follow your instincts. Do not be deterred by the fainthearted.
- Have faith in the greatness of your country and the armed forces that defend it.
- Never defer American leadership to supranational institutions such as the United Nations.
- Never underestimate the willingness and potential of strategic adversaries to launch attacks against U.S. interests and to exploit weaknesses in defensive positions.
- Always stand up to an aggressor and send a clear signal that acts of aggression will be punished.
- America's military must be prepared for the unexpected, even in times of apparent peace. A successful campaign can only be waged if the foundations have already been laid in terms of military investment. The Falklands War could not have been fought if Thatcher had not reversed defense cuts and rebuilt Britain's military capacity.

CHAPTER EIGHT

KEEPING AMERICA SECURE AND CONFRONTING TERRORISM

"There are in a sense no final victories, for the struggle against evil in the world is never ending."
—MARGARET THATCHER, MESSAGE ON
THE TWENTY-FIFTH ANNIVERSARY OF THE LIBERATION
OF THE FALKLANDS, JUNE 13, 2007[1]

The Importance of a Strong Defense

As the Falklands War, the Cold War, two Gulf wars, the war in Afghanistan, and the global War on Terror have amply demonstrated, a strong defense is vital both for deterring aggressors and in defeating them. Precautionary measures are also essential. As Margaret Thatcher observed, "Nowhere more than in defence and foreign policy does what I have come to consider 'Thatcher's law' apply—in politics the unexpected happens. You have to be prepared and able to face it."[2] She championed the principle that military build-ups prevent wars rather than start them, a point she forcefully made in an address to a joint session of Congress on a visit to Washington in 1985:

> Mr. Speaker, wars are not caused by the build-up of weapons. They are caused when an aggressor believes he can achieve his objectives at an acceptable price. The war of 1939 was not caused by an arms race. It sprang from a tyrant's belief that other countries lacked the means and the will to resist him. Remember Bismarck's phrase: "Do I want war? Of course not! I want victory!" Our task is to see that potential aggressors, from whatever quarter, understand plainly that the capacity and the resolve of the West would deny them victory in war and that the price they would pay would be intolerable.[3]

In a speech to Canada's Fraser Institute in 1993, Thatcher outlined the three key questions any hostile power will ask before launching an invasion of another country. The first is, "Has my adversary a strong defense?" The second is, can the adversary "get his forces to the scene of action required?" And the third is, "Has he, or she, the resolve?" On all three counts, Britain was prepared for the Falklands War, but Argentina's General Galtieri badly underestimated the resolve and fighting capability of the British. Both the retaking of the Falklands and the removal of Saddam Hussein from Kuwait, Thatcher said, were made possible by maintaining strong militaries:

> It was the first time in the post–Second World War world when an aggressor had been stopped, and the international law that you shall not take anyone else's territory or possessions had been upheld.
>
> Please note: it was not upheld by the United Nations, nor was getting Iraq out of Kuwait done by the United Nations; it

was done by lead nation states with a strong defence. And never let it be forgotten, in all my life in politics the unexpected has happened. The Falklands was the unexpected. Later, it was the Gulf. But at no time did I ever, I or President Reagan, or President Bush, have to think: have we got the requisite defensive weapons? Because wise foresight had seen to it that we had. Even when we cut down government expenditure, within the total I increased expenditure on defence; we were never prepared to let that go down. And I hope it's a lesson that people have learned.[4]

The Gutting of NATO Defense Spending

Defense spending, as in the 1970s, is now on the decline on both sides of the Atlantic. Only three members of the NATO alliance are currently meeting the agreed minimum defense spending of 2 percent of GDP—the United States, Britain, and Greece. French defense spending fell below the 2-percent benchmark in 2011. Sixteen European NATO members have reduced military spending since 2008, with cuts exceeding 10 percent in some cases. Luke Coffey of The Heritage Foundation, a former British Ministry of Defence special advisor, told Congress in April 2012, "To put this into perspective, with an annual budget of $4.5 billion, New York City spends more on policing than 13 NATO members spend on defense."[5] Outgoing U.S. Defense Secretary Robert Gates warned in his farewell address in Brussels in June 2011 that NATO is rapidly becoming a two-tier alliance, with American taxpayers now shouldering the cost of more than 75 percent of total NATO defense spending, an unsustainable arrangement. Future U.S. leaders, Gates said, "may not consider the return on America's investment in NATO worth the cost."[6]

Thatcher recognized that "the American people will be prepared to accept the burden of world leadership and to act as the international community's enforcer of last resort—but only if the U.S. can rely on the support of its allies."[7] Even the United Kingdom, which boasts a military tradition as illustrious as any in the world, is dramatically reducing its capabilities. The approach taken by Britain's Conservative-Liberal coalition government is the antithesis of Margaret Thatcher's in the 1980s.

British defense has been scaled back so severely that several former military commanders, including Admiral Sir John Forster Woodward, the head of the 1982 task force, believe that it might be impossible to retake the Falkland Islands today.[8] And Argentina's renewed aggressiveness makes the question more than academic. The regime of President Cristina Kirchner has attempted a partial maritime blockade, in some cases boarding European fishing vessels operating under Falkland Islands licenses and refusing to accept cruise ships headed for the Falklands. The increasingly unpopular president, struggling with mounting economic woes, has repeatedly demanded that the islands be handed over to her country and has issued several inflammatory statements attacking the United Kingdom. Her foreign minister, Héctor Timerman, has declared that the Falklands will be under Argentine control within twenty years and refuses to recognize the Falkland Islanders' right to self-determination.[9]

Kirchner is a bully like Galtieri, though without his military strength, and she is trying to intimidate the Falkland Islanders. Britain has strengthened the islands' defenses in recent years, but their situation is precarious. The Royal Navy's last aircraft carrier was recently decommissioned, and it is difficult to fight a war on the other side of the world without one. The Harrier fleet that was decisive in the 1982 conflict has been sold off, so even if the navy had a carrier, there might not be any aircraft to put on it. Defense cuts have also hurt the British army. By the end of the decade, the army will have just eighty-two thousand troops, "the smallest Army since the Napoleonic wars," according to General Sir Mike Jackson.[10]

America's Declining Defense Capability

The vulnerability of the Falkland Islands should be a warning to the United States about gutting our defenses. Unfortunately, the warning is going unheeded. The Obama administration has announced defense cuts of $500 billion over the next decade. These cuts are in addition to $330 billion of cuts to procurement programs in 2009, and a further $78 billion reduction in the Pentagon's budget in 2010.[11] Mackenzie Eaglen of the American Enterprise Institute offers a sobering assessment of these cuts: They are "the final nail in the coffin of our national contract with our all-volunteer military—that if they fight, they'll have the best to win. It marks the beginning of the end of America's unquestioned international military dominance. Our soldiers will increasingly go into combat with aged equipment, lacking assurance that they'll prevail against any enemy."[12]

America's armed forces are being forced to fight with badly outdated equipment. The average age of a U.S. strategic bomber is thirty-four years, and the average for tanker aircraft is forty-seven years. The U.S. fleet now numbers only 284 ships—the smallest it has been since 1916. The number of fighter squadrons now stands at just thirty-nine, compared with eighty-two at the end of the Cold War.[13] As a joint report of the American Enterprise Institute, The Heritage Foundation, and the Foreign Policy Initiative warned in July 2011, America is well on the way toward a "hollow" military equipped with the same aircraft, ships, tanks, and helicopters it was using at the end of the Cold War.[14]

America's military competitiveness is also being eroded by a decline in research and development. Spending on this critical component of national defense is less as a percentage of GDP than it was in the 1960s, and further cuts are planned. China's spending on military research and development, by contrast, is rising by more than 10 percent a year and will surpass that of the United States by 2023.[15]

There are worrying signs of isolationism in Washington, such as the Obama administration's plans to scale back America's long-standing military presence in Europe. In 2013 there were about eighty thousand U.S. military personnel at twenty-eight American bases across the Atlantic, down from roughly four hundred thousand in the early 1950s. The Pentagon plans to reduce America's troop strength in Europe by more than ten thousand troops, withdrawing at least two brigade combat teams by 2014.[16]

It is a serious mistake to dismiss U.S. bases in Europe as "Cold War relics." They are not intended to pick up the slack in Europe's defenses. They primarily serve as vital "forward operating bases of the twenty-first century," allowing the U.S. military to respond rapidly to crises in the Middle East and North Africa as well as the Caucasus.[17] These bases also strengthen the transatlantic alliance by demonstrating America's commitment to European security.

The NATO alliance had no greater advocate than Margaret Thatcher, who saw it as a "beacon of hope to the oppressed people of the Soviet bloc."[18] NATO's purpose was "to safeguard freedom, our common heritage and civilisation founded on the principles of democracy, personal liberty, and the rule of law."[19] It remains the foundation of transatlantic defense, and Americans ought to oppose attempts to weaken it, including French and German plans for developing a European Union defense identity in competition with NATO.

A Dangerous Path

The reductions in defense spending on both sides of the Atlantic are reckless and foolhardy. As Churchill warned in his Iron Curtain address, "It is in the years of peace that wars are prevented."[20] The cuts to the defense budget will barely make a dent in the federal budget deficit, which is driven overwhelmingly by the cost of entitlement programs. Defense cuts are a destructive feel-good exercise by the Left, which for decades has been pressing for America's military to have its wings clipped. As Thatcher noted in her address to the North Atlantic Assembly following victory in the Falklands, "If we were to sacrifice defense to the needs of the Welfare State, the day might come when we should have neither peace nor freedom nor be able to provide our people with the schools, the hospitals, and all the other elements of a modern, civilised state."[21]

Those who support the scaling back of the American armed forces should remember the pertinent advice that Thatcher shared just before she became prime minister: "We must look to our defences.... A household which finds itself short of money, and then goes and cancels its insurance policies, courts disaster. So a nation which skimps on its defences is playing with fire. We shall rebuild our defences and in so doing strengthen the alliance. That must be a prime task for the new Conservative Government in the years which lie ahead. Most of these things the great majority of our people believe."[22]

Confronting the Terrorist Threat

Few leaders in modern times have had the direct, personal experience of terrorism that Margaret Thatcher had. She understood that terrorists "are the enemies of civilized society everywhere,"[23] a great evil to be crushed and vanquished, "a threat to freedom both savage and insidious."[24] The threat of terrorism was always in the background during her years in Downing Street, and she remained its most forceful opponent, never conceding that terrorists should get their way by using force to advance political causes.

Thatcher confronted the scourge of terrorism in May 1980, soon after becoming prime minister, when six gunmen forced their way into the Iranian Embassy in London and held more than twenty people hostage, including a policeman and two BBC journalists. She ordered the Special Air Service (SAS) to storm the embassy. All the surviving hostages were freed (one had been murdered before the raid began), and five gunmen were shot dead, with one captured. There were no SAS losses. As Thatcher recalled, "We had sent a signal to terrorists everywhere that they could expect no deals and would extort no favours from Britain."[25]

Thatcher's government fought a sustained campaign against the Provisional Irish Republican Army (IRA), which, on a number of occasions, launched terrorist attacks on mainland Britain. Lady Thatcher and her husband themselves narrowly escaped death in one of these, the bombing of the Grand Hotel in Brighton during the 1984 Conservative Party conference. The blast claimed five lives, among them Conservative MP Sir Anthony Berry, and injured thirty-four others, including the employment secretary, Norman Tebbit, and his wife, Margaret. Thatcher described the attack in her memoirs: "At 2.54 a.m. a loud thud shook the room. There were a few seconds' silence and then there was a second slightly different noise, in fact created by falling masonry. I knew immediately that it was a bomb—perhaps two bombs, a large followed by a smaller device—but at this stage I did not know that the explosion had taken place inside the hotel.... Those who had sought to kill me had placed the bomb in the wrong place."[26]

Despite the carnage around her, the prime minister was determined not to allow the terrorists to succeed in intimidating the British people. She refused to leave Brighton (about fifty miles from London) for Downing Street and insisted on staying the night in a local police college[27] and delivering her conference speech that morning. As she forcefully told her audience of Conservative Party faithful, "It was an attempt not only to disrupt and terminate our Conference; it was an attempt to cripple Her Majesty's democratically elected Government. That is the scale of the outrage in which we have all shared, and the fact that we are gathered here now—shocked, but composed and determined—is a sign not only that this attack has failed, but that all attempts to destroy democracy by terrorism will fail."[28]

This unflinching courage was characteristic of Thatcher's leadership. The IRA had struck just months before, setting off a bomb in the midst of Christmas shoppers at Harrods in London. Five people, including two policemen, were killed. "I shall never forget the sight of the charred body of a teenage girl," Thatcher recorded in her memoirs, "lying where she had been blown against the store window."[29]

Even worse was to come. Four years later, in 1987, an IRA bomb exploded at a Remembrance Day service in Enniskillen, in Northern Ireland. Eleven people were killed and sixty injured in an act of unspeakable barbarism. Soon after this massacre, Thatcher reminded the British people that they must never give in to terrorism: "There can be no compromise with terrorism. Treating with terrorists can only lead to more bombings, more violence, more people murdered. The best defence against terrorism is to make clear that you will never give in."[30]

In addition to a wave of attacks on civilian and military targets during Thatcher's premiership, the IRA murdered her close friend and fellow MP Ian Gow with a car bomb in 1990. The attack brought back painful memories of the death of another dear friend and MP, Airey Neave, who was assassinated in 1979 by the Irish National Liberation Army. The breakaway faction of the IRA managed to place a bomb under his car in the House of Commons garage. The deaths of Neave and later Gow only strengthened Thatcher's determination to stand up to terrorism. As she later recalled, "No amount of terror can succeed in its aim if even a few outspoken men and women of integrity and courage dare to call terrorism murder and any compromise with it treachery."[31]

The Rise of Islamist Terrorism

Since Thatcher left office, a new terrorist threat has largely eclipsed that of the Irish Republicans. Islamist terrorism is now the primary challenge for Britain's intelligence and security services. In the aftermath of the 9/11 attacks on New York and Washington, D.C., she recognized immediately what the West was facing—nothing less than a war against an Islamist enemy that seeks the destruction of the free world. In Washington in 2002, she outlined exactly what was at stake in the years ahead and offered advice to President George W. Bush:

> We still confront today a twin-headed monster of terrorism and of proliferating weapons of mass destruction. And both those heads must be removed if the beast itself is to be destroyed. Evil, it is true, has always been with us. But evil was never so technically sophisticated, never so elusive, never so devoid of scruple, and never so anxious to inflict civilian casualties. The West must prevail—or else concede a reign of global lawlessness and violence unparalleled in modern times.[32]

Margaret Thatcher was among the first British politicians to address the Islamist threat and warn the West of the perils of appeasing it. She sharply criticized Islamic clerics in Britain who had not done enough to condemn the 9/11 attacks in America, which took the lives of sixty-seven Britons. In a column for the *New York Times* in February 2002, she compared the Islamist threat to Bolshevism, a dangerous ideology that had to be confronted and defeated on a global level:

> Islamic extremism today, like Bolshevism in the past, is an armed doctrine. It is an aggressive ideology promoted by

fanatical, well-armed devotees. And, like Communism, it requires an all-embracing long-term strategy to defeat it....

The events of Sept. 11 are a terrible reminder that freedom demands eternal vigilance. And for too long we have not been vigilant. We have harbored those who hated us, tolerated those who threatened us and indulged those who weakened us.[33]

As was so often the case, Margaret Thatcher was years ahead of her peers in pointing out the threat of Islamist terrorism. Unlike most British politicians, she identified the enemy without hesitation—Islamists who seek the destruction of Britain, the United States, and the West. It was not until the July 7, 2005, al Qaeda suicide attacks on the London public transport system (commonly known as the 7/7 attacks), which claimed fifty-two lives and injured seven hundred, that Britain's political leaders began to fully grasp the scale of the threat, not only from foreign jihadists coming into the country from places such as Pakistan and Iraq but, more important, from home-grown Islamist extremists, some of whom were second- or third-generation British subjects and who in many ways posed an even greater threat.

British intelligence believes there are two thousand al Qaeda sympathizers in the United Kingdom.[34] Between 2001 and 2008, more than 1,400 persons were arrested for terrorism-related offenses in Britain,[35] and the threats continue.[36] The United States also faces a threat from domestic Islamist extremists. At least fifty terror plots against U.S. targets have been prevented in the post-9/11 era.[37]

The West is facing what has been termed a "long war" against terrorism,[38] one that will be waged for decades to come, both on the home front and across the globe, from Afghanistan and Pakistan to Mali and Somalia. It will ultimately be won with strength and determination like Margaret

Thatcher's. "The terrorist threat to freedom is worldwide," she said. "It can never be met by appeasement. Give in to the terrorist and you breed more terrorism. At home and abroad our message is the same. We will not bargain, nor compromise, nor bend the knee to terrorists."[39]

Key Leadership Lessons

- Freedom must always be protected through a strong defense. Military weakness only invites attack.

- America must have a modern, properly funded military capable of defending the homeland and projecting might on the world stage in support of U.S. interests.

- Increase defense spending and invest for the future. Never reduce long-term military capability—America's competitors, especially China, will not.

- Always be prepared for an unexpected war. There is no room for complacency.

- NATO must remain at the heart of the transatlantic alliance. The United States should resist European efforts to erode NATO.

- The United States must maintain its commitment to basing American troops in Europe, not only to advance the transatlantic partnership but for vital strategic interests, including the ability to deploy forces rapidly to the Middle East and North Africa.

- Never give in to terrorism. There can be no compromise with those who seek to advance their goals through the use of violence.

- The Islamist terrorist threat must be clearly identified and emphatically defeated.

CHAPTER NINE

AMERICA MUST LEAD

"I am an undiluted admirer of American values...
and I believe they will continue to inspire not just
the people of the United States but millions upon millions
across the face of the globe."
—MARGARET THATCHER, SPEECH TO
THE ASPEN INSTITUTE, COLORADO, AUGUST 5, 1990[1]

America's Greatness

Sometimes Americans have to be reminded of their own country's greatness by outsiders. Non-Americans from Alexis de Tocqueville to Sir Winston Churchill have eloquently expressed what today's liberal elites will never say—that this is a truly great, exceptional nation whose love of liberty is an inspiration to the rest of the world. It was Churchill, the son of an American mother and an English father, who asked with tears in his eyes on a visit to New York as prime minister in 1952, "What other nation in history, when it became supremely powerful, has had no thought of territorial aggrandizement, no ambition but to use its resources for the good of the world? I marvel at America's altruism, her sublime disinterestedness."[2]

Margaret Thatcher shared Churchill's enthusiasm for the United States, the engine of the free world. As she put it in *Statecraft*, "America is more than a nation or a state or a superpower; it is an idea—and one which has transformed and continues to transform us all. America is unique—in its power, its wealth, its outlook in the world."[3] She was always full of admiration for the American people, once describing them as "the most generous, hospitable people the world over."[4]

American leadership has been greatly strengthened by the partnership with Great Britain. The "Special Relationship," as it is commonly known, has been at the heart of British and American foreign policy since World War II, when it was forged by Winston Churchill and Franklin D. Roosevelt. It is undoubtedly the world's most powerful bilateral partnership, based on the deep trust between two great nations. The defense, intelligence, diplomatic, and cultural ties between the United States and the United Kingdom are the envy of the world. The Special Relationship reached its apogee when Margaret Thatcher was prime minister and Ronald Reagan was in the White House.

A chief goal of Thatcher's premiership was to advance the Special Relationship. Without the alliance with America, British power and influence would be limited. It was always Thatcher's view that "the primary objective of British foreign policy [is] to seek to preserve and strengthen not only the special relationship between Britain and America but also the Atlantic Alliance as a whole."[5] At the same time, America cannot lead as the world's superpower alone. She reminded an audience of American foreign policy experts in Los Angeles in 1991, "Even America cannot be truly safe and secure in isolation."[6] Two years later, she explained the basis of the partnership: "More than any other country, Britain shares America's passionate commitment to democracy and willingness to stand and fight for it."[7]

At the heart of Thatcher's solicitude for the Anglo-American alliance was her belief in the unity of the "English-speaking peoples," drawing inspiration from Churchill's declaration that "we must never cease to proclaim in fearless tones the great principles of freedom and the rights of Man which are the joint inheritance of the English-speaking world...."[8] Addressing the English-Speaking Union in New York just before the end of the millennium, Thatcher affirmed, "The fact is, the English-speaking peoples are, above all others, uniquely situated to impart these lessons of liberty to those who seek to emulate our successes. We boast, after all, the world's oldest systems of representative government; we were the first to recognise fundamental rights and individual liberties; and we have preserved our institutions of freedom for centuries, often against overwhelming odds."[9]

Few British politicians have spent more time on American soil than Margaret Thatcher. Her first visit was in 1967 as a guest of the State Department's International Exchange Program. She and her husband spent six weeks traveling across the country. She was, at the time, the front-bench Opposition spokesman for treasury and economic affairs, and her meetings took her far beyond Washington to Atlanta, Houston, San Francisco, Los Angeles, Omaha, Chicago, and finally New York.[10] It was the beginning of Thatcher's close association with the world's superpower, one that would span more than four decades and continue in her role as patron of The Heritage Foundation in Washington, D.C. The foundation established the Margaret Thatcher Center for Freedom in 2005, the only such center in the world that bears her name, and which is dedicated to advancing the partnership between the United States and Great Britain.

Thatcher returned to Washington in 1975, this time as leader of the Opposition. She was received at the White House by President Gerald Ford and also held meetings with Secretary of State Henry Kissinger, Treasury Secretary William E. Simon, and Defense Secretary James Schlesinger. The trip immediately boosted her standing at home, forcing her critics within the Conservative Party to think again before dismissing her rise to power as a "temporary fluke."[11] In her first major speech in the United States, at the National Press Club, she spoke of her affinity with the simple, frugal "puritan morality of the founders of America," pointing out that she "was not brought up to prosperity. Hard work was the only way. We did not live wasteful, slothful or indolent lives but struggled to live a worthwhile life more rewarding in every sense. It is a moral struggle … the morality of work, of self-sacrifice, of trying to do the right thing at whatever the cost."[12] This was also, she said, the morality of capitalism, and she proclaimed that "the period of high spending and slack thinking is over."

Four years later, Thatcher was back at the White House, this time as British prime minister, the guest of Jimmy Carter in the midst of the Iran hostage crisis. In remarks at her arrival ceremony, she described the United States as "the most powerful force for freedom and democracy the world over" and conveyed a message of solidarity with the American people.[13] There were, however, considerable ideological differences between the new conservative British government and the distinctly liberal American administration. Carter's America, as Thatcher later recalled, was a super-power that "had suffered a terrible decline of confidence in its role in the world," a decline that was soon to be reversed.[14] Although she personally liked Carter and considered him a good friend to her and to Britain, she was sharply critical of his lack of vision and his unwillingness to stand up to communism. "He was in some ways personally ill-suited to the presidency," Thatcher wrote in her memoirs, "agonizing over big decisions and too concerned with detail…. In leading a great nation decency and assiduousness are not enough."[15]

Know Who Your Friends Are

Margaret Thatcher was the first Western European leader President Reagan invited to the White House. The 1981 meeting was facilitated by his close friend and counselor, Edwin Meese III, and her visit to Washington instantly revived the Special Relationship.[16] On her arrival, she told the president, "We in Britain stand with you.... In Britain you will find a ready response, an ally, valiant, staunch and true."[17] During an exchange of toasts at the White House dinner, she promised Reagan that when he visited her country, he would find the friendship of the British people and that "the years of socialist bumbling are at an end."[18] Reagan in turn offered a moving tribute to the country of Churchill the following evening at a dinner given by the British ambassador:

> The British people, who nourish the great civilized ideas, know the forces of good ultimately rally and triumph over evil. That, after all, is the legend of the Knights of the Round Table, the legend of the man who lived on Baker Street, the story of London in the Blitz, the meaning of the Union Jack snapping briskly in the wind. Madam Prime Minister, I'll make one further prediction, that the British people are once again about to pay homage to their beloved Sir Winston by doing him the honor of proving him wrong and showing the world that their finest hour is yet to come, and how he would have loved the irony of that. How proud it would have made him.[19]

This was not the two leaders' first meeting, of course. That had occurred in 1975, when Reagan, on a visit to England, was introduced to Thatcher soon after she had taken the helm of the Conservative Party. Reagan recorded his vivid memory of that meeting in his autobiography: "I'd planned on spending only a few minutes with Margaret Thatcher but we ended up talking for almost two hours. I liked her immediately—she was warm, feminine, gracious, and intelligent—and it was evident from our first words that we were soul mates when it came to reducing government and expanding economic freedom."[20]

Reagan went on to describe his response to a haughty Englishman who had mocked the very idea of "a woman prime minister," reminding him that "England once had a queen named Victoria who did rather well."[21] Thatcher was similarly impressed by Reagan in their first meeting, recalling that she was "immediately won over by his charm, sense of humour and directness." She had admired the California governor since her husband had introduced her to one of his speeches in the late 1960s. Thatcher felt a natural affinity for a leader who, like herself, had come from outside of the political elite and had been dismissed by his detractors as, in her words, "a right-wing maverick."[22] They were outsiders from humble backgrounds who had been sneered at from the upper echelons of their own parties. And both were politicians with a deft common touch, a natural ability to relate to ordinary voters across all classes on issues that voters cared about.

It was the beginning of a spectacularly successful partnership that sparked a transatlantic economic revolution and brought down a tyrannical empire. It was a true meeting of the minds between two highly principled conservative politicians dedicated to the renewal of their respective nations. As Thatcher recalled in *The Downing Street Years*, "I knew that I was talking to someone who instinctively felt and thought as I did; not just about policies but about a philosophy of government, a view of human nature, all the high ideals and values which lie—or ought to lie—beneath any politician's ambitions to lead his country."[23]

Thatcher was elated by Reagan's 1980 victory over Carter, staying up until three o'clock in the morning listening to election broadcasts from the United States.[24] She recognized that the election was historic, marking the return of self-confident American leadership. Reagan's ascendancy was also an opportunity for Britain to stand with America once again, united in the advance of liberty, and she called his inauguration "a symbol of hope for the Alliance."[25] In a 1988 article for *National Review*, she wrote of her conviction upon Reagan's election "that together we could tackle the formidable tasks before us: to get our countries on their feet, to restore their pride and their values, and to help create a safer and better world."[26] For Thatcher, her joint mission with the new president was clear:

> Both Ronald Reagan and I deliberately set out to reverse state control, liberate individual initiative and stand up to a Soviet Empire which was every bit as evil as he described it—and a great deal more serious threat to our way of life than today's revisionists pretend. His main task lay in foreign and defence policy—which was only natural for a superpower. My main task was in economic affairs —to roll back collectivism in all its forms. This included, of course, a campaign against communism everywhere—the most total tyranny in the world.[27]

Without the strength of the Reagan-Thatcher partnership, there would not have been an economic recovery in the United States or Great Britain, the military might of the West would have further declined, the NATO alliance might have withered away, the Soviet empire could have survived for decades more, Eastern Europe would have continued toiling under Communist rule, and Washington and London would have been the capital cities of fading powers. In addition, the Argentine flag would be flying over the Falklands, and the hammer and sickle would be holding sway over large parts of Latin America and Africa. Indeed, the world today would likely be a very different place, with freedom in retreat and the forces of totalitarianism in ascendancy.

There were occasionally frank disagreements between Reagan and Thatcher, what she liked to call "family" squabbles, such as her unhappiness over the American invasion in 1983 of Grenada, a member of the British Commonwealth. But this was a period of Anglo-American unity,

cemented by the closest political relationship between any two international leaders in modern times. The cordial relations between their com-
paratively low-key successors, John Major and George H. W. Bush, did
not match the Reagan-Thatcher friendship. Tony Blair provided invaluable—and politically costly—support to George W. Bush in the War on
Terror, but the alliance between those two men was limited to the war.
They did not share political beliefs on other matters of importance. And
there is nothing about the relations between Barack Obama and David
Cameron that could be called a "partnership."

Thatcher's loyalty to Reagan, as a friend and ally, is legendary. On a
visit to the United States during the Iran-Contra hearings on Capitol
Hill—the low point of his presidency—Thatcher delivered a robust
defense of the beleaguered president on *Face the Nation*, rebutting any
suggestion that America's credibility or influence had been weakened. She
memorably told her interviewer, Leslie Stahl, "Cheer up! America is a
strong country with a great president, a great people and a great future!"
She reprimanded Stahl for suggesting that "our credibility has been shred-
ded," asking her, "Why are you doing your level best to put the worst foot
forward? Why?" She concluded her interview by saying: "I beg of you, you
should have as much faith in America as I have!" By any measure, it was
an extraordinary exchange. It was also an example of great leadership from
a conviction politician who never hesitated to identify liberal nonsense
when she was confronted with it.[28] After the interview, the British embassy
in Washington was besieged with phone calls from American viewers
eager to congratulate Thatcher for her words of support for their president. Thatcher herself received a call from Reagan expressing his gratitude,
with long and loud applause in the background from members of his
cabinet.[29]

Reagan stepped down from public life eighteen months later, leaving
the American superpower in far better shape than he had found it. He

invited Thatcher to the White House in November 1988 as his last official guest. At the arrival ceremony, he thanked his great friend for her steadfast support, noting that "in the critical hour, Margaret Thatcher and the people of Great Britain stood fast in freedom's defense and upheld all the noblest of your island's traditions; yours was the part of courage and resolve and vision." In response, the British prime minister spoke of how America stood tall in the world once again thanks to Reagan's leadership. The American president had "restored faith in the American dream—a dream of boundless opportunity built on enterprise, individual effort and personal generosity."[30]

Loyalty Matters

The episode that demonstrated most dramatically Thatcher's commitment to the Anglo-American bond was her support of the U.S. raid on Tripoli in 1986. It was also an important lesson in leadership, for her loyalty aroused fierce domestic and international criticism. It also put the world's dictators on notice that attacks on the United States and its allies would have consequences.

On April 5, 1986, a bomb exploded in a West Berlin discotheque popular with U.S. servicemen. Two Americans were killed and another two hundred persons, sixty of them Americans, were injured. It quickly became clear that Libya was responsible. Colonel Gaddafi, the country's dictator, had become notorious for his sponsorship of terrorism, and President Reagan was determined to teach him a lesson.

Reagan swiftly requested permission to fly American F-111 warplanes out of Britain for a strike on Libya. Thatcher agreed, and on April 15, 1986, just ten days after the Berlin attack, the United States carried out a wave of air strikes against military targets in Tripoli, flying from the Royal Air Force base at Lakenheath in Suffolk. Thatcher was alone among European leaders in directly supporting the Libya operation,[31] and her decision took tremendous political courage. Germany's chancellor, Helmut Kohl, made it clear in advance of the raid that the United States could not count on the backing of Europe. France refused to allow the F-111s to fly across its airspace, and Spain insisted that the planes could not pass over its territory if there was any risk of their being noticed. The fighters eventually bypassed Spain, flying through the Strait of Gibraltar.

The raid on Tripoli destroyed a number of key targets but also killed some civilians. It was strongly condemned across much of the world, including by the Labour and Liberal parties in Britain. Thatcher came under heavy fire in the House of Commons for her support for President Reagan, with one MP declaring she had "the blood of innocents on her hands" and that "she should divorce herself from Reagan's Rambo policies."[32] Another MP sneeringly accused her of inviting more terrorist attacks on Britain, because of "her passionate political infatuation with Reagan [that] is leading her to the misjudgments of a giddy girl."[33] Neil Kinnock, the Labour leader, called on the House of Commons to "condemn the United States action," claiming that it had "caused bloodshed and damage to innocents."[34]

Undaunted by her critics, Thatcher launched a robust defense of her support for the American action. "Terrorism has to be defeated," she told the Commons. "Terrorism attacks free societies and plays on those fears. If those tactics succeed, terrorism saps the will of free peoples to resist." The partnership with America had preserved peace in Europe for nearly forty years. America's war, Thatcher declared, was Britain's war too:

> The United States is our greatest ally. It is the foundation of the Alliance which has preserved our security and peace for more than a generation. In defence of liberty, our liberty as well as its own, the United States maintains in Western Europe 330,000 service men. That is more than the whole of Britain's

regular forces. The United States gave us unstinting help when
we needed it in the South Atlantic four years ago.... The time
had come for action. The United States took it. Its decision was
justified, and, as friends and allies, we support it.[35]

Thatcher showed the kind of mettle that is all too rare. The attacks
came not only from the Opposition, the media, and much of Europe, but
from within her own party. As she recalled in her memoirs, she had "faced
down the anti-Americanism which threatened to poison our relations
with our closest and most powerful ally, and not only survived but
emerged with greater authority and influence on the world stage: this the
critics could not ignore."[36] This was leadership at its finest, and an example for conservatives on both sides of the Atlantic. Ronald Reagan, for one,
appreciated it: "I have never known of a time when the English bulldog
is safer than it is with Margaret Thatcher."[37]

"No Time to Go Wobbly"

Margaret Thatcher stood with the United States one last time in the
late summer of 1990, three months before she stepped down as prime
minister. On August 2, Iraq invaded and occupied Kuwait. Thatcher, who
happened to be in Colorado with President Bush to address an Aspen
Institute conference, immediately dispatched two British warships to the
Gulf and then met with the president. Aggressors, she told him, must
never be appeased and had to be confronted.[38] In a press conference following their meeting, the two leaders demanded the withdrawal of Saddam Hussein's army from Kuwait. "Prime Minister Margaret Thatcher
and I are looking at it on exactly the same wavelength," said Bush.[39]

In her Aspen speech three days later, Thatcher condemned Iraq's invasion of Kuwait, warning that "if we let it succeed, no small country can
ever feel safe again. The law of the jungle would take over from the rule

of law."[40] For the Iron Lady, this was a clear-cut battle between good and evil: "In the annals of injustice," she said later, "Saddam Hussein had descended to depths of wickedness and brutality we thought never to see again."[41] The Iraqi tyrant was not "mad," but "totally calculating, brutal, and having no regard whatsoever for the dignity or rights of the individual.... He has no regard for human life or liberty or justice."[42]

As Washington planned the huge military buildup that eventually led to Saddam's humiliating defeat in February 1991, Thatcher was at the heart of U.S. decision making. She was invited to participate in a key meeting in Washington at the White House following the Aspen conference, which included President Bush, Vice President Dan Quayle, National Security Advisor Brent Scowcroft, Secretary of State James Baker, and Bush's chief of staff, John Sununu. In Thatcher's words, "I was never taken into the Americans' confidence more than I was during the two hours or so I spent that afternoon at the White House."[43]

Until this point, the relationship between Bush and Thatcher had been nowhere near as close as that between Reagan and Thatcher. The end of the Reagan era had ushered in a new approach in Washington, one less focused on relations with Britain. "With the new team's arrival in the White House," wrote Thatcher, "I found myself dealing with an Administration which saw Germany as its main European partner in leadership.... I felt I could not always rely as before on American cooperation." The Gulf War, however, was a wake-up call for the Bush White House, which swiftly realized that Britain was America's most reliable, trusted, and important ally:

> Anglo-American relations suddenly lost their chill; indeed by
> the end they had hardly been warmer.... This change of heart
> was confirmed by the aggression of Saddam Hussein against
> Kuwait which shattered any illusion that tyranny had been

everywhere defeated. The UN might pass its resolutions; but there would soon be a full-scale war to fight. Suddenly a Britain with armed forces which had the skills, and a government which had the resolve, to fight alongside America, seemed to be the real European "partner in leadership."[44]

Thatcher played a major role in the creation of what eventually became the largest coalition of nations assembled for a military operation since World War II, with thirty-four countries taking part. Britain provided more than thirty thousand military personnel for Operation Desert Storm, in contrast to many of America's European allies (with the notable exception of France), who failed to pull their weight. She was credited with stiffening Washington's own resolve when she famously told George H. W. Bush that it was "no time to go wobbly" in the early days of the Gulf crisis, urging the president to interdict every Iraqi shipping vessel heading for Oman, without exception.[45] She also counseled against a deferential approach to the United Nations, which, during the Falklands War, had been all too eager to push for endless negotiations in an effort to stall military action. As she later noted, "I did not like unnecessary resort to the UN, because it suggested that sovereign states lacked the moral authority to act on their own behalf.... There was still no substituting for the leadership of the United States."[46]

The liberation of Kuwait was testimony to the strength of American and British world leadership, and above all, the willingness of the world's superpower to act at a time of crisis, with a military that had been rebuilt during the Reagan years. It was, as Thatcher remarked just months after the liberation, "not fought by the UN," but by "sovereign nations under the leadership of the United States of America, who came together to enforce its Resolutions."[47] The United Nations can never be a substitute for American leadership. "If we attempt to rely solely on the United

Nations," Thatcher warned, "we shall soon learn that it is an institution where copious resolutions become a substitute for effective action."[48]

The Gulf War was also a symbol, like the Cold War, of the West's determination to stand up to tyranny. Without the resolve of Margaret Thatcher and George H. W. Bush, Saddam Hussein would have retained control of Kuwait, threatened Saudi Arabia, and probably sparked a broader regional war. As Thatcher pointed out when she received the Presidential Medal of Freedom at a White House ceremony in March 1991, "Like you, Mr. President, I hate violence. And there's only one thing I hate even more—giving in to violence. We didn't give in to it. The battle of Desert Storm has not only liberated Kuwait and her people; it has sent an awesome warning to any other dictator who sets out to extinguish the rights of others for his own evil gain. The sanction of force must not be left to tyrants who have no moral scruples about its use."[49]

Alliances Matter

The Libyan strike, Operation Desert Storm, and the later wars in Iraq and Afghanistan all demonstrated the fundamental importance of the Special Relationship. On Libya, while the rest of Europe refused to back America, Britain, under Thatcher's leadership, stood with her. Time and again, from World War II to the recent NATO-led campaign to remove Colonel Gaddafi from power, British forces have fought alongside their American allies.

Great Britain was the first country to join the United States in the war against the Taliban in the wake of the 9/11 attacks. When the United States went into Iraq and removed Saddam Hussein from power in 2003, Britain gave its full support to Operation Iraqi Freedom, sending forty-five thousand ground troops while much of the rest of western Europe stood on the sidelines. Many of Europe's big powers, including France and Germany, opposed U.S. intervention. While fair-weather friends did their best to mock and even impede America's war effort, Britain stood shoulder to shoulder with the United States. For this, the former prime minister Tony Blair deserves credit, despite the vitriol directed at him by opponents of the war.

Blair's economic policies and much of his domestic agenda (not to mention his stance on Europe) left much to be desired, but he was right on the War on Terror and was a steadfast ally of President George W. Bush, a point that Thatcher remarked upon in a speech in Washington in December 2002 when she accepted the Clare Boothe Luce Award from Vice President Cheney. "I am also proud," she told her audience, "that Britain stands where we must always stand—as America's surest and staunchest ally. Prime Minister Blair and I are, as is well known, political opponents. But in this vital matter I salute his strong, bold leadership."[50] After her death, Blair acknowledged Thatcher's support and advice on this and other foreign policy issues, stating that "as a person she was kind and generous spirited and was always immensely supportive to me as Prime Minister although we came from opposite sides of politics."[51] The Iraq War showed that alliances matter. As Thatcher declared in a major speech to the Chicago Council on Global Affairs in June 1991,

> Whatever people say, the special relationship does exist, it does count and it must continue, because the United States needs friends in the lonely task of world leadership. More than any other country, Britain shares America's passionate commitment to democracy and willingness to stand and fight for it. You can cut through all the verbiage and obfuscation. It's really as simple as that.

The Anglo-American alliance, so deeply cherished by Margaret Thatcher and Ronald Reagan, has been frayed in recent years. The intelligence links, the defense cooperation, and the economic investment are still there, but at a political and leadership level, there is no denying that the Special Relationship has been eroded since George W. Bush left the White House in January 2009. Much of the blame for this weakening of the alliance must be placed at the feet of Barack Obama, who in the opening days of his presidency communicated his attitude toward Great Britain in a symbolic gesture.

The British government had loaned a beautifully crafted bronze bust of Winston Churchill to President Bush after the 9/11 terrorist attacks on New York and Washington, D.C., as a sign of solidarity with the American people. President Obama had the option of retaining the bust but instead sent it back to the British embassy. The British press interpreted the return of the bust as a snub. It was an early sign that relations would be very different under the new administration.

This episode was followed by a less-than-warm White House reception for British prime minister Gordon Brown in April 2009. Obama's ceremonial gift to the prime minister communicated the new president's disregard—twenty-five DVDs, ranging from *Toy Story* to *The Wizard of Oz*, which could not even be played in Britain due to regional DVD coding. A senior State Department spokesman explained the frosty treatment of Mr. Brown to a reporter from the London *Sunday Telegraph*: "There's nothing special about Britain. You're just the same as the other 190 countries in the world. You shouldn't expect special treatment."[52]

These words symbolize the Obama administration's approach to Britain throughout its first term—condescension, contempt, and at times sheer animosity. President Obama himself made no secret of his extraordinary view that France is America's strongest ally in a joint press conference with French president Nicolas Sarkozy,[53] and he seemed to delight in the U.S. government's extremely aggressive campaign against the United Kingdom's largest company, British Petroleum, in the wake of the Gulf oil spill. The White House pledged to put a "boot on the throat" of the oil giant, helping to wipe out about half of its share value, directly affecting the pensions of eighteen million Britons. This even prompted London's mayor, the usually pro-Obama Boris Johnson, to call for an end to "anti-British rhetoric" as well as "buck-passing and name-calling" by the Obama administration.[54]

When tensions between London and Buenos Aires over the Falkland Islands began to rise again at the start of the decade, Anglo-American relations deteriorated further. A vote of the inhabitants of the Falklands in March 2013 established that 99.8 percent of the population desires to remain British. Yet the Obama administration has supported President Kirchner's calls for UN-brokered negotiations over the sovereignty of the Falklands. Hillary Clinton was vocal as secretary of state in her support for Kirchner's demands,[55] and the State Department approved a series of resolutions by the Organization of American States urging the same. In a further insult to the United Kingdom (as well as to the Falkland Islanders themselves), the Obama administration has even insisted on referring to the islands by the Argentine name, the "Malvinas."

President Obama's shabby treatment of Great Britain is an object lesson in how not to treat a close friend and ally. He has disregarded one of Margaret Thatcher's chief principles—maintaining strong alliances. In a speech titled "The Sinews of Foreign Policy" given in Brussels in 1978 while she was still the leader of the Opposition, she said, "Foreign policy commitments are not to be made and unmade at will. We are bound by past commitments. We have a respect for past contracts, both as governments and as ordinary citizens. We cannot expect others to keep their word to us unless we keep our word to them."[56]

Never Apologize for America

Some of the countries that the Obama administration has treated worst are among America's closest friends and allies. At the same time,

Obama has done his best to curry favor with his country's adversaries and strategic competitors. He began his presidency by delivering a series of groveling apologies for America's supposed historical sins. In Strasbourg, he told an audience of French and Germans that "America has shown arrogance, and been dismissive, even derisive," in its approach towards Europe, undoubtedly referring to tensions over the Iraq War and the War on Terror.[57] Weeks later, in May 2009, he delivered his infamous Cairo address, taking another swipe at the Iraq War and condemning his own nation's treatment of Islamist terror suspects in the wake of the 9/11 attacks, practices which were, in his view, "contrary to our traditions and our ideals."[58] To loud applause, Barack Obama also pledged to close the prison at Guantanamo (a promise that would prove to be empty). Obama had earlier issued an apology to the entire Muslim world in an interview with *Al Arabiya*, stating that "we sometimes make mistakes. We have not been perfect."[59] He also made a series of other apologies across the world, including to the Summit of the Americas in Port of Spain, Trinidad and Tobago,[60] and to the Turkish parliament in Istanbul, where he spoke of "our own darker periods in our history."[61]

This world apology tour, which Obama mistook for leadership, has had its parallels across the Atlantic. Labour prime ministers, including Tony Blair, have been quick to apologize for Britain's imperial past. Margaret Thatcher's rule, however, was always to take pride in your country's history and achievements and to never apologize for its greatness. She was always unflinching, for example, in her view that the British Empire was a force for good. In a 1983 speech to the Winston Churchill Foundation, she reminded her audience that "we in Great Britain have given freedom and independence to more than 40 countries whose populations now number more than one thousand million—a quarter of the world's total."[62] Indeed, no other empire in history has relinquished power with such grace as the British Empire.

The world's largest democracy, India, was directly ruled by Britain for nearly a century. British rule bequeathed to India a civil service, legal system, education system, and infrastructure that are the envy of southern Asia. It is not a coincidence that four of the world's five freest economies and six of the world's ten freest are English-speaking former colonies of the British Empire. Hong Kong, Singapore, Australia, New Zealand, and Canada lead the globe in economic freedom and are among the most prosperous nations in the world.[63] Their success is due in large part to their distinctly British foundations—the rule of law, limited government, and a free-enterprise system. The historian Andrew Roberts notes that the economies of the English-speaking world account for more than a third of global GDP despite accounting for only 7.5 percent of the world's population.[64]

America Must Lead the Free World

Margaret Thatcher, with John Winthrop, always believed that America is a shining "city upon a hill," a land of freedom and opportunity. There is simply no alternative to American leadership. In Thatcher's words, "In the modern world, only the United States has the capacity and the generosity of spirit to lead on the required scale."[65] It is unimaginable to think of a world dominated by China, with its disregard for human rights, its disdain for personal liberty and freedom, and its rejection of the values that underpin a free society. Or a world where America becomes another EU, submerged in government regulation, suffocated by supranationalism, and militarily weak.

The free world owes America an immense debt for all it has done to advance and defend freedom across the globe. With good reason, Margaret Thatcher referred to the American commitment to freedom as "the lynchpin of the West."[66] The amount of hatred and anger directed at the world's superpower is matched only by the selflessness of the American people and their willingness to stand up for the values of the Founding Fathers. It is only because of America's momentous sacrifice of blood and treasure over the last hundred years that Europe is free today, that Soviet communism is consigned to museums and history books, and that the forces of tyranny and terror are held at bay.

As Thatcher reminded her audience in a speech before a joint meeting of the U.S. House and Senate in February 1985, "America has been the principal architect of a peace in Europe which has lasted forty years." Recalling a service of thanksgiving in the spring of 1945, when the German guns had finally fallen silent, the Iron Lady spoke of the debt owed by Europe to the United States:

> On this day, close to the fortieth anniversary of that service and of peace in Europe—one of the longest periods without war in all our history—I should like to recall those words and acknowledge how faithfully America has fulfilled them. For our deliverance from what might have befallen us, I would not have us leave our gratitude to the tributes of history. The debt the free peoples of Europe owe to this nation, generous with its bounty, willing to share its strength, seeking to protect the weak, is incalculable. We thank and salute you![67]

In more recent times, U.S. forces have liberated tens of millions from tyranny in Iraq and Afghanistan, sweeping aside barbaric regimes that have murdered and brutalized their own people. The world is a far better place without the likes of Saddam Hussein and the Taliban in power, with their torture chambers, terrorism, and savagery.

Thatcher pointed out on numerous occasions throughout her public life that "America's duty is to lead; the other Western countries' duty is to support its leadership." American leadership, she believed, is vital to

the preservation of Western civilization, a cause of the utmost importance to the entire world. As she told an audience in Washington in
December 1997:

> Provided Western countries unite under American leadership,
> the West will remain the dominant global influence; if we do
> not, the opportunity for rogue states and new tyrannical pow
> ers to exploit our divisions will increase, and so will the danger
> to all.
>
> So the task for conservatives today is to revive a sense of
> Western identity, unity and resolve. The West is after all not just
> some ephemeral Cold-War construct: it is the core of a civiliza
> tion which has carried all before it, transforming the outlook
> and pattern of life of every continent. It is time to proclaim our
> beliefs in the wonderful creativity of the human spirit, in the
> rights of property and the rule of law, in the extraordinary
> fruitfulness of enterprise and trade, and in the Western cultural
> heritage without which our liberty would long ago have degen
> erated into license or collapsed into tyranny.
>
> These are as much the tasks of today as they were of yes
> terday, as much the duty of conservative believers now as they
> were when Ronald Reagan and I refused to accept the decline
> of the West as our ineluctable destiny.[68]

Her message has lost none of its urgency. America must lead the free
world in the defense of liberty against a host of threats, from the rogue
regimes of Iran and North Korea and strategic adversaries like Russia and
China to the global tide of Islamist militancy. It can best do this through
its partnership with Great Britain and with a NATO alliance whose members carry their weight. The United States must spurn the temptations of

isolationism, for without American leadership, the forces of tyranny will prevail, ultimately endangering the prosperity and security of the United States.

Key Leadership Lessons

- The Anglo-American alliance is vital to the defense of the free world. The preservation of the Special Relationship should always be a top foreign policy priority for conservative leaders.

- Always stand with your allies and keep them close. Remind your international friends that they matter. Distinguish between fair-weather friends and those who shed blood on the battlefield alongside American forces.

- Leading from behind is a policy of defeat. This should never be the ethos of a superpower.

- Never allow the United Nations to wield a veto over the foreign policy of the United States. The UN can sometimes be useful for advancing American interests, but it is no substitute for American leadership.

- Never apologize for America. This projects weakness and a lack of resolve. The only beneficiaries of this approach are America's enemies.

- Never be afraid to defend American exceptionalism, both at home and abroad. It is a message that should be given from Cincinnati to Cairo.

- Have faith in America. This is a great nation with an incredible spirit of enterprise and liberty, a beacon of hope to the world. No nation has sacrificed more for the cause of freedom in modern times than the United States.

- There is no alternative to American leadership on the world stage. Without American leadership, the world is a far more dangerous place. Isolationism will empower those who seek to harm America.

CHAPTER TEN

THE TEN PRINCIPLES
OF SUCCESSFUL
CONSERVATIVE
LEADERSHIP

"We don't say back to the centre ground. We say,
stand on your principles like a rock."
—MARGARET THATCHER, ADDRESS TO
CONSERVATIVE PARTY ACTIVISTS, OCTOBER 16, 1981[1]

I n a speech to the Conservative Women's conference in 1989, toward the end of her time as prime minister, Margaret Thatcher took pride in declaring that "we in the Conservative Party are conviction politicians. We know what we believe. We hold fast to our beliefs. And when elected, we put them into practice."[2] Thatcher's conviction was fundamental to her success as Britain's longest continuously serving prime minister of the twentieth century. As she put it to fellow members of Parliament, "We never put power before principles."[3]

Adherence to one's convictions is one of the key principles that Thatcher followed throughout her career, principles that are essential for successful conservative leadership today at every level of government. They also apply to conservative business leaders, whether they are captaining a Fortune 500 company or operating a small business with twenty employees. America needs strong conservative leadership, in both government and the private sector. Because the Iron Lady gave such a splendid example of how it is done, her guiding principles are worth reflecting on.

1. Walk with Destiny and Serve a Higher Purpose

Throughout her political life, Thatcher was driven by a sense of purpose, a clear sense of destiny, and a deep-seated patriotism. "Our supreme loyalty is to the country and the things for which it stands," she reminded the British people in 1979.[4] Her mission as prime minister was never in doubt—to save her country from socialist-driven decline and to stand up for freedom in the face of tyranny. On both fronts she succeeded, changing the course of history for the British nation and, with Ronald Reagan, bringing down a monstrous empire of tyranny.

The example she tried to follow was that of Churchill during World War II, who was to a great degree her role model in this regard, shaping her sense of resolve and determination. She said that Churchill "was the man of that hour, a true figure of destiny, and himself profoundly conscious of the fact." In a tribute to Churchill at Blenheim Palace, Thatcher quoted his own account of the day in May 1940 when he became prime minister at one of the most perilous moments in his country's history: "[When] I went to bed at about three a.m. I was conscious of a profound sense of relief. At last I had the authority to give directions over the whole scene. I felt as if I were walking with destiny, and all my past life had been but a preparation for this hour and for this trial."[5]

This sense of mission and destiny, of living for a higher purpose, distinguishes a great leader from a mediocre one. Thatcher, Churchill, and Reagan all possessed it, yet it is largely absent from the seats of power in Washington and London today. Today's generation of conservative leaders needs to recapture the spirit of these great figures if the world's superpower is to be revived and America is to be saved from decline. Margaret Thatcher always thought big, with the future of her nation at heart. She may have come from a small village in Lincolnshire, but her outlook and vision were on a grand scale, driven by selflessness and sacrifice for country. As she declared in a speech to the General Assembly of the Church of Scotland, "There is little hope for democracy if the hearts of men and women in democratic societies cannot be touched by a call to something greater than themselves."[6]

2. Lead with Conviction

Margaret Thatcher was, above all, a conviction politician. Even her fiercest critics would acknowledge that she was driven by unshakeable beliefs. "It is the half-hearted who lose—it is those with conviction who carry the day," she insisted.[7] Without courage and conviction, Thatcher noted as a newly elected MP for Finchley, "the others are hollow and useless."[8] She learned courage and conviction, she said, "in a small town [from] a father who had a conviction approach."[9]

The notion that steely conviction is a fault in a leader seemed ridiculous to the Iron Lady: "There would have been no great prophets, no great philosophers in life, no great things to follow, if those who propounded the views had gone out and said 'Brothers, follow me, I believe in consensus.'"[10] Consensus for its own sake is the preoccupation of the feeble and the faint of heart. It has no place in true leadership. "What great cause would have been fought and won under the banner 'I stand for consensus'?"

she asked in a speech in Australia in 1981. "To me consensus seems to be—the process of abandoning all beliefs, principles, values and policies in search of something in which no-one believes, but to which no one objects—the process of avoiding the very issues that have to be solved, merely because you cannot get agreement on the way ahead."[11]

3. Stick to Core Conservative Ideas

It is no coincidence that Thatcher won three successive general elections and never lost one. She firmly stuck to conservative principles and advanced a consistent message that voters understood. The British electorate knew what they were getting with Margaret Thatcher, and they rewarded her with unprecedented success. She stood for limited government, free enterprise, privatization, low taxation, strong defense, and an unyielding opposition to socialism. She was a champion of small businesses, declaring war on red tape and burdensome regulations, and an enemy of big government and the heavy hand of bureaucracy.

In order to win the war of ideas, conservatives have to be clear in their message and confident of their values. There is always the temptation to "soften" the message, to "reinvent" the brand, to bend and reshape central principles in order to appeal to different sections of society. The British Conservative Party has given in to this temptation in recent years, a mistake that cost it an outright majority in the 2010 general election (winning only 36 percent of the vote) and forced it into a coalition with the Liberal Democrats. Shortly after Thatcher's death, the current leader of her party, David Cameron, assured an interviewer that he is not a "Thatcherite."[12] He is also not the leader of a majority party.

A conservative party must not sacrifice its principles in pursuit of popularity. Eighteen months after becoming prime minister, Thatcher insisted that "the worst betrayal the British people could suffer at the hands of this Government would be for us to seek a little more popularity now by sacrificing all hope of future stability and prosperity. That is not our way."[13] In 1987, after her third consecutive triumph at the national polls, Thatcher showed the spirit that was the secret to her success:

> Remember how we had all been lectured about political impossibility? You couldn't be a Conservative, and sound like a Conservative, and win an election—they said. And you certainly couldn't win an election and then act like a Conservative and win another election. And—this was absolutely beyond dispute—you couldn't win two elections and go on behaving like a Conservative, and yet win a third election. Don't you harbor just the faintest suspicion that somewhere along the line something went wrong with that theory?[14]

4. Understand the Grassroots

Margaret Thatcher was able to lead her country for eleven years because she understood the beating heart of the British people. She was in touch with "Middle England," the traditional conservative values of the typical British voter, concerned with bread-and-butter issues like the economy, taxes, law and order, immigration, and the quality of public services. As Thatcher noted in the second year of her premiership, "Those who seek to govern must be willing to allow their hearts and minds to lie open to the people."[15]

Like Ronald Reagan in the United States, she was not from the metropolitan elite. As a grocer's daughter, Thatcher understood the needs and concerns of hard-working, ordinary people trying to make ends meet, often under the most difficult of circumstances. In her own words, "Thatcherism didn't start with Thatcher. I pulled everything that was best out of the character of a people, everything that was commonsense and everything that was courage. And that is really how it works."[16]

She appealed not only to middle-class voters, but also to large sections of the working class, who benefited from lower taxes and the selling of millions of council houses (public housing), which greatly boosted home ownership in Britain. Thatcherism managed to win over large cross sections of society because of its truly aspirational nature, offering an opportunity for less well-off voters to share in Britain's new economic prosperity through purchasing their own homes and buying shares in newly privatized companies. At the beginning of Margaret Thatcher's premiership, there were just three million private shareholders in Britain. By the end of it, that figure had risen to more than eleven million. During the same period, the percentage of Britons who owned their own homes rose from 55 to 63 percent.[17]

While politicians of the Left stirred up resentment between different class and economic groups, Thatcher envisioned a country united by common principles where economic freedom fostered opportunity and achievement. Socialism is the politics of division, fear, and loathing, appealing to the worst instincts of humanity. In contrast, as Thatcherism demonstrated, the free-enterprise system appeals to man's nobler instincts, to his desire to be creative and work hard and to advance prosperity through individual initiative and limited government. Thatcher's first party conference speech as prime minister in 1979 was a call to unite the country, urging the British people to "remember that we are a nation, and that a nation is an extended family.... At times like these, the strength of the family is truly tested. It is then that the temptation is greatest for its members to start blaming one another and dissipating their strength in bitterness and bickering. Let us do all in our power to see one another's point of view and to widen the common ground on which we stand."[18]

5. Be Courageous

"Courage," Margaret Thatcher once said, "is what you show in the heat of the battle, not at the post-mortem."[19] When running for high office, American presidential candidates are invariably asked how they will respond to that "three a.m. call," the moment when a leader must respond to a crisis with fortitude and boldness. That moment came for George W. Bush with the 9/11 attacks on Washington and New York. He rose to the occasion by swiftly launching Operation Enduring Freedom to remove the Taliban from power in Afghanistan and hunt down the terrorists of al Qaeda. Rudy Giuliani also responded with true grit, inspiring a nation to fight back against Islamist terrorism and recover from the biggest assault on American soil since Pearl Harbor. Who can forget the sight of New York's mayor walking through the dust-covered, debris-strewn streets of lower Manhattan, leading the city's rescue efforts on a day that three thousand people lost their lives at the hands of a barbaric enemy?

"There will be times when the unexpected happens," Margaret Thatcher said of moments like these. "There will be times when only you can make a certain decision."[20] She demonstrated that fearlessness herself when Argentina invaded the Falklands, and again when she confronted the power of Britain's trade unions during the miners' strike of 1984–85. Her leadership in the face of trade union militancy was vital in rescuing the country from its economic paralysis.

But Thatcher's courage was more than just political. She also displayed tremendous personal courage when the IRA tried to assassinate her in 1984. Not even a terrorist bomb, which narrowly missed killing her in her hotel in Brighton, could keep her from delivering her address to the Conservative Party conference just a few hours later. The IRA taunted her that day: "Today we were unlucky, but remember, we only have to be lucky once; you will have to be lucky always."[21] She took no heed of this kind of intimidation and led a sustained British military campaign against Irish Republican terrorists that made them understand that they would gain nothing through a campaign of mass murder. As Thatcher remarked four years later in a speech to women leaders, "The ultimate virtue is courage, the ultimate, the only thing you have got left sometimes—courage and fellowship."[22]

6. Be Decisive

Political courage and decisiveness go hand in hand, as Margaret Thatcher's leadership during the Falklands War showed. It is often forgotten that the British task force that sailed eight thousand miles across the world had been assembled within forty-eight hours. Her decision to launch a liberation force at such short notice was an act of extraordinary leadership, and it carried huge risks. It is important to bear in mind that Britain's last major military operation had taken place during the Suez crisis nearly thirty years earlier and had provoked a national crisis of confidence. There can be no doubt that the failure of the Falklands mission would have been a national calamity, big enough to bring down the Thatcher government. It also would have scarred the British nation for a generation, deepening the sense of post-imperial decline. "But I had *total faith* in the professionalism, and in the loyalty and morale of the British armed forces," said Thatcher,[23] and that faith proved to be justified.

Thatcher's decisiveness in sending the task force was matched by the soundness of her instincts during the conduct of the war itself. Her decision to sink the Argentine cruiser *Belgrano* was the kind of determined quick thinking that results in victory during wartime. There can be no doubt that if she had not acted immediately, many more British lives would have been lost, and the war would have been significantly prolonged.

7. Be Loyal

On June 11, 2004, Lady Thatcher paid tribute to her great friend Ronald Reagan, delivering a eulogy for the American president at his state funeral in Washington's National Cathedral. Advised by her doctor against speaking publicly, she recorded remarks that were delivered by video link in the service. In her moving testimonial to President Reagan's leadership, she declared that "the world mourns the passing of the great liberator and echoes his prayer: God bless America." Reagan, she said, had "inspired America and its allies with renewed faith in their mission of freedom," and had won the Cold War "without firing a shot."[24]

Thatcher's tribute to Reagan was so powerful because every word came from the heart of a leader who had stood with him through adversity. Loyalty mattered to Margaret Thatcher, and the strength of the Reagan-Thatcher partnership is unlikely to be matched in our time. Thatcher stood with Reagan not only against the Soviet Union but also against the Libyan dictator Gaddafi.

The relationship was not a one-way street; Ronald Reagan frequently gave his support and encouragement to Thatcher. As Thatcher makes clear in her memoirs, without America's military backing during the Falklands War, Britain would not have been able to defeat Argentina and liberate the islands. The close ties between the White House and Downing Street enhanced Thatcher's influence on the world stage. The world is a far better place, and a safer one, thanks to the strength of the Anglo-American alliance, a partnership that depends upon shared interests and values as well as upon on the principle of loyalty between leaders on opposite sides of the Atlantic. For Margaret Thatcher, loyalty was essential to successful leadership. As she put it in a press conference in Washington in 1988, "Loyalty is a very positive quality. If you cannot give it yourself, you should not be entitled to expect to receive it from others."[25]

8. Know Your Brief and Prepare

"Work is interesting: I enjoy it," Margaret Thatcher told her Russian audience on Soviet television on a visit to Moscow in 1987. Thatcher was famous for requiring only five hours of sleep, and she had a well-earned reputation for being an incredibly hard-working politician. After a punishing schedule of eight to ten political engagements a day, she would usually start work on ministerial papers at ten o'clock every night. Her breakfast consisted of a cup of black coffee and two vitamin C supplements, while lunch was a bowl of clear soup and a portion of fruit.[26]

Margaret Thatcher's opponents could disagree with her message, criticize her ideas, and condemn her policies, but they could rarely find fault with her command of the facts, her knowledge of her brief, and the power of her delivery. She took pride in being exceptionally well informed on the details of government policy and the issues that her administration faced, no matter how complex or seemingly unimportant. Parliament can be an extremely unforgiving environment. She noted at the beginning of her career there, "In the House of Commons, no matter what the subject under debate, there is always someone who knows it inside out, and who will pick up any half-true statement."[27] The separation of the executive and legislative branches of the United States government shields the American president from direct questioning by members of Congress. In contrast, a British prime minister is expected to face questions from members of Parliament every week when the House is in session—twice a week when Thatcher was prime minister. This requires an extraordinary mastery of many subjects, often with little time to acquire it. Thatcher was a formidable debater, as a series of Labour leaders found when they faced her across the dispatch box.

She was also meticulous in her preparation for speeches and television interviews. Major speeches were carefully rehearsed to ensure that every line was delivered with the right tone and emphasis. Thatcher was a naturally gifted orator with a tremendous talent for appealing to the hearts of her audience. But even the greatest public speakers also depend on practice for successful delivery, a lesson that every conservative politician and businessman should heed. There is no substitute for good preparation, and no room for overconfidence, no matter how familiar the speaker is with the topic. A stumbling statement, factual error, or weak message can undercut any political candidate or business leader. In some cases it can even finish someone's career.

9. Make Your Message Clear

Margaret Thatcher was one of the most successful communicators of the modern era. She could present complex issues in a way that most voters could easily understand. Few politicians in the last sixty years—perhaps only Ronald Reagan and John F. Kennedy—could rival her as a public speaker. She never hid her own admiration for President Reagan's extraordinary talent for communicating big ideas to ordinary voters, once remarking that "his fundamental instincts are the instincts of most decent, honourable people in democracy—that is why they felt such a sympathy with him—and then he could communicate."[28]

Thatcher's speeches, interviews, and statements, like Reagan's, always conveyed a clear-cut message. Her 1980 speech to the Conservative Party conference was a case in point, with her delivery of one of the most memorable lines in recent British history. Addressing the party faithful, she confidently declared, "To those waiting with bated breath for that favourite media catchphrase, the 'U' turn, I have only one thing to say. 'You turn if you want to. The lady's not for turning.'"[29] With a single turn of phrase, she projected resolve and determination and sent a signal that her free-market revolution was here to stay.

That speech powerfully reinforced her image as the "Iron Lady," which she had earned in 1976 at Kensington Town Hall.[30] Her "Britain Awake" speech, delivered as leader of the Opposition, had sent shock-waves through the other side of Europe. Her warnings against a Soviet Union bent on "world dominance" forced the Russians to take the measure of a formidable new adversary. The speech made Thatcher, still three and a half years away from governing, an international figure. It also projected Cold War leadership at a time when there was little of it coming from either London or Washington. It was a sequel to Churchill's landmark "Iron Curtain" speech and a precursor to Reagan's 1983 "Evil Empire" speech. It was one of the few speeches in history that have threatened an empire and compelled the grudging respect—even admiration—of its rulers.

Great speeches rely on brilliant lines, and often on gifted speechwriters. But they will always ring hollow if they are not matched by a clear set of beliefs and a leader who delivers them with conviction. They can also defy conventional wisdom, as Thatcher demonstrated in her Bruges speech in 1988, where she challenged decades of thinking on Europe, calling for a Europe of sovereign nation states as opposed to a European superstate. Her address to the College of Europe[31] is the most important speech on the future of the continent delivered by a European leader in the last three decades, fundamentally altering the European debate. It was also years ahead of its time, making arguments that seemed controversial. When Prime Minister David Cameron delivered a similar speech[32] in London in February 2013, explaining why Europe needed to change, he was merely walking in Thatcher's footsteps.

The "lady's not for turning," "Britain Awake," and the Bruges speeches shaped the course of history. They succeeded because the message was compelling and based on a core set of beliefs. They were spoken from the heart by a truly great communicator who understood the importance of delivering a clearly defined message.

10. Deliver a Message of Hope and Optimism

Margaret Thatcher's put-downs of her political adversaries are legendary. In hundreds of appearances at the House of Commons dispatch box during prime minister's questions sessions, she shattered the egos of countless MPs. Her speeches were also filled with devastating critiques of Britain's socialist Opposition as well as its bankrupt ideology, broadsides that frequently brought the house down at party conferences.

In the arena of political combat, Margaret Thatcher had no equal in 1970s and 1980s Britain. But Thatcher's speeches were also replete with messages of hope and optimism for the future. They were invariably positive in tone, offering a brighter future for the British people. Her words were frequently inspirational, focused on national renewal and the restoration of British greatness. The rejection of national decline was her constant theme as a candidate for prime minister, presenting an overwhelmingly bright, conservative vision for the future.

In 1977, the high-water mark of British socialism, Thatcher promised "a new renaissance matching anything in our island's long and outstanding history." To an audience of skeptical bankers and economists at the Zurich Economic Society, she said, "I have reason to believe that the tide is beginning to turn against collectivism, statism, dirigism, whatever you call it. And this turn is rooted in a revulsion against the sour fruit of socialist experience."[33] Thatcher ended by quoting Rudyard Kipling, one of her favorite writers, from his 1911 poem "The Dawn Wind":

> So when the world is asleep, and there seems no hope of her waking

Out of some long, bad dream that makes her mutter and
moan,
Suddenly, all men arise to the noise of fetters breaking,
And everyone smiles at his neighbour and tells him his soul is
his own![34]

It must have been hard for her audience in Switzerland to imagine the
sick man of Europe, drowning in a sea of socialism and debt, becoming
an economic powerhouse. But it did just that a few years later under
Thatcher's leadership. There is much for American conservatives today
to learn from Thatcher's spirit of optimism. Like Reagan, she was uncom-
promising in her condemnation of left-wing ideology, but she frequently
joined harsh words with a theme of renewal. In politics it is essential to
point out and illustrate the flaws and follies of your opponents. As
Thatcher demonstrated, it is also vital to present an alternative based on
conservative ideas that an electorate can understand.

The depth of despair and economic ruin in 1970s Britain was a
national humiliation. Thatcher's message of hope seemed to many, both
at home and abroad, an impossible dream. But she succeeded in turning
her country around, drawing upon an extraordinary faith in the human
spirit and the principles of liberty that sustain it.

CONCLUSION

"You always have people who take the soft option.
The apparently easy way out is the way that gets you into
deepest trouble. The lesson is, you don't soften fundamental
principles. You positively push them forward into the future."
—MARGARET THATCHER, "DON'T UNDO MY WORK,"
NEWSWEEK, APRIL 27, 1992[1]

In a 1988 television interview, David Frost asked Margaret Thatcher if she thought there would ever be another male prime minister in Britain. She responded, "I think male prime ministers one day will come back into fashion!"[2] There have been four prime ministers (all men) since she left office in 1990, but none has matched her achievements. Thatcher was a political titan whose principles and ideals continue to inspire the defenders of freedom all over the globe.

The world is a far better place because of the leadership of the grocer's daughter from Grantham. Thatcher won three general elections not by shifting her policies, adapting her ideology, or compromising her beliefs, but by sticking to clearly defined conservative principles.

The Iron Lady did not lead by pandering to the latest political fashions, appealing to special interest groups, or, as Barack Obama famously put it on the campaign trail, getting "revenge."[3] Her political vision was unwavering, based on principles not fads. It was also unfailingly optimistic. People will succeed, she believed, with hard work if you let them.

Her greatest achievements as prime minister included trimming the power of the state while empowering the individual, reversing Britain's decline, and helping to bring down an evil empire in Europe. She reminded the world that the role of government is to serve the people, not to lord over them.

"Nothing is beyond this nation. Decline is not inevitable," Thatcher told an exuberant crowd at the Conservative Party conference in 1981.[4] But she also reminded her countrymen that the flame of liberty can be extinguished if a complacent nation lacks the will to keep it alive. Soon after becoming prime minister, she warned that "constant vigilance must be our aim" because "liberty's survival can never be taken for granted: ground held or gained by one generation can easily be lost in the next."[5]

Not only did Margaret Thatcher restore her own country's belief in itself, but she also helped restore America's too. Newt Gingrich, the former Speaker of the House of Representatives, explains: "Margaret Thatcher was the forerunner who made Reagan possible. The 1979 campaign was the direct model from which we took much of the 1980 Republican campaign. Reagan drew great strength from Thatcher, and her courage and toughness in living through that first recession and toughness in the Falklands War rallied Americans in a remarkable way."[6]

Thatcher's partnership with Reagan proved central to the downfall of communism and the revitalization of Western leadership following the decline of the Carter years and the despondency of the post-Vietnam era. With good reason, Reagan described his British counterpart as "a tower of strength and a solid friend of the U.S."[7] Not since Churchill had a world leader placed so much faith in the ideal of American leadership and invested so heavily in the transatlantic partnership. Through many difficult moments, not least during the American raid on Libya in 1986,

Thatcher provided the encouragement and support that the United States needed. "The Anglo-American relationship is not some out-dated romantic notion," Thatcher insisted. "It reflects shared history, language, values and ideals—the very things which generate the willingness for sacrifice on which the outcome of every military venture ultimately depends."[8]

Perhaps no leader in modern times has had such an unshakable belief in the greatness of the United States, the spirit of its people, and its ability to lead. As Thatcher put it, the United States is "the greatest country in the free world, a country born to be free,"[9] one with "an awesome responsibility."[10]

But today America's leadership has been weakened by a dangerous lurch to the left, one that threatens its standing as the world's superpower. After several years of piling up debt, restricting economic freedom, expanding the welfare state, raising taxes on wealth creators, tangling businesses in red tape, and saddling the country with Obamacare, one of the most ill-conceived and destructive government programs in history, the United States is in serious trouble. America's deep defense cuts and its foreign policy of weakness and appeasement have caused many to question its ability to lead.

America urgently needs to return to the values and principles upon which it was founded. It must cherish again the ideals of free enterprise and individual freedom. Together with Ronald Reagan, there is no better role model for a conservative revival in America than Margaret Thatcher. "We fought not just for power," she said, "we fought for our true beliefs— and we were really quite successful. We were successful at home—transforming our economies and liberating the energy of our people. We were successful abroad—bringing to bear the full force of freedom against the socialism which had pledged to bury it."[11]

Thatcher showed how courage, conviction, and a willingness to fight for conservative policies can prevail, even in the most difficult circumstances.

Those who believe that victory can be achieved only through compromise and adaptation should learn from Thatcher's tremendous record of success. It makes no sense for today's conservatives to adopt a platform that mimics the policies and language of the Left. Sacrificing core conservative values to appeal to the center ground or even to liberal voters is a recipe for failure. In the words of the Iron Lady, speaking in Washington soon after Britain's socialists had regained power in 1997, "Nothing would be more foolish than for conservatives to seek refuge in aping our opponents' policies, rhetoric, or—heaven forbid—even identity. After all, if people really want social democracy they won't be voting for us conservatives in any case."[12]

The next few years will be crucial for the future of conservatism in America. Today's conservative leaders have much to learn from Thatcher's example—not just her policies, but the way in which she advanced and delivered them, as well as the consistency of her message. Thatcher was never interested in her personal popularity. She simply believed that "policies must be in line with principles.... Far better to command respect for doing the right thing long-term than to pursue short-term popularity."[13]

Senator Ted Cruz of Texas reminded Americans of Thatcher's wisdom when he quoted one of her bedrock principles: "First you win the argument, then you win the vote."[14] Speaking to American conservatives, Thatcher warned them to resist "the oldest temptation that conservative parties face. That is the desire to be what we are not—in search of expressions of approval from those who are our sworn ideological adversaries, while showing a reluctance to listen to our proven friends."[15]

Conservatism can triumph again in America. But it requires leaders with the courage and conviction of Margaret Thatcher and Ronald Reagan. The stakes could not be higher for the United States and the free world. As Thatcher warned, "The decline of the West has been predicted

before, and it has not occurred. It need not occur. And it will not occur—
if we conservatives keep faith in everything we have achieved and the
bedrock principles which inspired us to prevail."[16]

ACKNOWLEDGMENTS

The authors are indebted to Harry W. Crocker, vice president and executive editor of Regnery, Marji Ross, Regnery's president and publisher, and Jeff Carneal, president of Eagle Publishing, who have overseen the production and publication of this book. It was Harry's idea for a book on Margaret Thatcher and leadership, one that would inspire the American conservative movement based on the ideals of a great champion for liberty. At Regnery, Tom Spence was our superb and always cheerful editor who worked tirelessly to ensure that everything went smoothly with the manuscript while applying tremendous attention to detail.

Erica Munkwitz provided invaluable assistance with the research for this book, and her indefatigable and always enthusiastic approach was admirable. A gifted scholar of British history at American University, Erica demonstrated a truly Thatcherite work ethic combined with an in-depth knowledge of the source material. Luke Coffey, the Margaret Thatcher

Fellow at The Heritage Foundation, read through drafts of the manuscript and provided extremely helpful advice on foreign and defense issues.

This book could not have been written without the support of Frank Swain and the Thatcher Foundation in Washington, D.C., as well as the encouragement of Mark Worthington, director of Lady Thatcher's Private Office. *Margaret Thatcher on Leadership* draws heavily from hundreds of speeches and interview transcripts compiled by Christopher Collins and contained in the Thatcher Foundation online archive, the most impressive and formidable archive of its kind in the world. Andrew Riley, the brilliant archivist of the Thatcher Papers at Churchill College, Cambridge, researched and provided many of the photographs featured in this book, and his help is greatly appreciated.

NOTES

Introduction

1. Margaret Thatcher, "Speech to Conservative Party Conference," Brighton, England, October 14, 1988, transcript, Margaret Thatcher Foundation, http://www.margaretthatcher.org/document/107352.

2. "Half of Voters Say Obama or Romney Embodies Their Views," Gallup Poll, November 2, 2012, http://www.gallup.com/poll/158477/half-voters-say-obama-romney-embodies-views.aspx.

3. Tess Stynes, "Circulation up at *Journal*, *Times*," *Wall Street Journal*, May 1, 2013, http://online.wsj.com/article/SB10001424127887324482504578454693739428314.html.

4. For example, this year's Netroots Nation, an annual convention for progressives, attracted three thousand attendees, while this year's CPAC had ten thousand attendees. See Dave Weigel, "Netroots Nation First Impressions," *Slate*, June 21, 2013, http://www.slate.com/blogs/weigel/2013/06/21/netroots_nation_first_impressions.html; and "Conservative Activisits Outline Political Future at CPAC Meeting," PBS *Newshour*, March 15, 2013, transcript, http://www.pbs.org/newshour/bb/politics/jan-june13/cpac_03-15.html.

5. Thatcher, "Speech to Conservative Party Conference," Brighton, England, October 14, 1988.

Chapter 1

1.   Margaret Thatcher, "The New Renaissance," speech to Zurich Economic Society, Switzerland, March 14, 1977, Margaret Thatcher Foundation, http://www.margaretthatcher.org/document/103336.

2.   Margaret Thatcher, "The Principles of Thatcherism," speech, Seoul, South Korea, September 3, 1992, transcript, Margaret Thatcher Foundation, http://www.margaretthatcher.org/document/108302.

3.   Will Stewart, "Revealed: Red Army Colonel Who Dubbed Maggie the Iron Lady … and Changed History," *Daily Mail* (London), February 24, 2007, http://www.dailymail.co.uk/news/article-438281/Revealed-Red-Army-colonel-dubbed-Maggie-Iron-Lady---changed-history.html.

4.   Ibid.

5.   Margaret Thatcher, *The Path to Power* (New York: HarperCollins, 1995), 362.

6.   Stewart, "Revealed: Red Army Colonel Who Dubbed Maggie the Iron Lady … and Changed History."

7.   Margaret Thatcher, "Britain Awake (The Iron Lady)," speech at Kensington Town Hall, Chelsea, England, January 19, 1976, transcript, Margaret Thatcher Foundation, http://www.margaretthatcher.org/document/102939.

8.   Ibid.

9.   Paul Kengor, "The Jimmy Carter Chronicles," *American Spectator*, February 18, 2011, http://spectator.org/archives/2011/02/18/the-jimmy-carter-chronicles.

10.   Thatcher, "Britain Awake."

11.   Ibid.

12.   Thatcher, *The Path to Power*, 362.

13.   Margaret Thatcher, "Speech to Finchley Conservatives," Selborne Hall, Southgate, England, January 31, 1976, transcript, Margaret Thatcher Foundation, http://www.margaretthatcher.org/document/102947.

14.   Margaret Thatcher, "Speech to Conservative Rally in Birmingham," Town Hall, Birmingham, England, April 19, 1979, transcript, Margaret Thatcher Foundation, http://www.margaretthatcher.org/document/104026.

15.   Margaret Thatcher, "The Trade Unions," General Election Press Conference, Conservative Central Office, Smith Square, Westminster, England, April 20, 1979, transcript, Margaret Thatcher Foundation, http://www.margaretthatcher.org/document/104029.

16.   Margaret Thatcher, "Speech to Conservative Rally in Birmingham," April 19, 1979, transcript, Margaret Thatcher Foundation, http://www.margaretthatcher.org/document/104026.

17. Jon Swaine, "Tory Party Conference: Margaret Thatcher Voted 'Greatest Tory,'" *Daily Telegraph* (London), September 30, 2008, http://www.telegraph.co.uk/news/politics/conservative/3107265/Tory-party-conference-Margaret-Thatcher-voted-greatest-Tory.html.

Chapter 2

1. Margaret Thatcher, "Speech to Conservative Party Conference," Blackpool, England, October 14, 1983, transcript, Margaret Thatcher Foundation, http://www.margaretthatcher.org/document/105454.

2. Andrew Pierce, "The Ultimate Eighties Revival Night," *Times* (London), October 14, 2005, http://www.margaretthatcher.org/document/110597.

3. Ronald Reagan, "Reagan's Speech at the 1994 Gala, on the Occasion of His 83rd Birthday," February 3, 1994, transcript, http://reagan2020.us/speeches/RNC_Gala.asp.

4. "Lady Thatcher Unveils Portrait of Herself and President Reagan by Mark Balma," YouTube video, from the unveiling in Washington, D.C., uploaded November 22, 2010, accessed April 30, 2013, http://www.youtube.com/watch?v=vw30WnuUlms.

5. Margaret Thatcher, "Speech Receiving Honorary Degree from University of Tel Aviv," London, England, July 7, 1986, transcript, Margaret Thatcher Foundation, http://www.margaretthatcher.org/document/106444.

6. Margaret Thatcher, "Speech Accepting an Honorary Degree from Hofstra University," New York, March 27, 2000, transcript, Margaret Thatcher Foundation, http://www.margaretthatcher.org/document/108387.

7. Ibid.

8. Margaret Thatcher, "The Principles of Thatcherism," speech, Seoul, South Korea, September 3, 1992, transcript, Margaret Thatcher Foundation, http://www.margaretthatcher.org/document/108302.

9. Ibid.

10. Ibid.

11. Ibid.

12. Margaret Thatcher, "Remarks on Becoming Prime Minister (St Francis's Prayer)," London, England, May 4, 1979, transcript, Margaret Thatcher Foundation, http://www.margaretthatcher.org/document/104078.

13. Margaret Thatcher, *The Path to Power* (New York: HarperCollins, 1995), 568.

14. Margaret Thatcher, "Speech to Scottish Conservative Party Conference," Aberdeen Exhibition and Conference Centre, Scotland, May 12, 1990, transcript,

Margaret Thatcher Foundation, http://www.margaretthatcher.org/document/108087. See also Margaret Thatcher, "Speech to the First International Conservative Congress," Washington, D.C., September 28, 1997, transcript, Margaret Thatcher Foundation, http://www.margaretthatcher.org/document/108374.

15. Margaret Thatcher, interview by David Frost, TV-AM, December 30, 1988, transcript, Margaret Thatcher Foundation, http://www.margaretthatcher.org/document/107022.

16. Thatcher, *The Path to Power*, 5.

17. Ibid., 566.

18. Ibid., 4.

19. Ibid., 19.

20. Howard Peters, "The Iron Lady," *ChemistryWorld*, May 1, 2012, http://www.rsc.org/chemistryworld/2012/05/iron-lady.

21. Margaret Thatcher, *The Downing Street Years* (New York: HarperCollins, 1993), 21.

22. Thatcher, *The Path to Power*, 4.

23. Ibid., 565.

24. Ibid.

25. Ibid., 566.

26. Thatcher, "The Principles of Thatcherism."

27. Ibid.

28. Thatcher, *The Path to Power*, 31. Italics in original.

29. Robin Harris, *Not For Turning: The Life of Margaret Thatcher* (London: Bantam Press, 2013), 445.

30. Margaret Thatcher, interview by Brian Walden, *Weekend World*, January 16, 1983, transcript, Margaret Thatcher Foundation, http://www.margaretthatcher.org/document/105087.

31. Margaret Thatcher, "Speech to Finchley Young Conservatives," December 7, 1985, originally published in *Finchley Times*, December 12, 1985, public statement, Margaret Thatcher Foundation, http://www.margaretthatcher.org/document/106194.

32. Margaret Thatcher, interview by Peter Riddell, *Financial Times*, November 23, 1987, Margaret Thatcher Foundation, http://www.margaretthatcher.org/document/106969.

33. Niall Ferguson, *Empire: The Rise and Demise of the British World Order and the Lessons for Global Power* (New York: Basic Books, 2002), xxi, 303.

34. Thatcher, *The Path To Power*, 21.

35. Margaret Thatcher, "Liberty and Limited Government," Keith Joseph Memorial Lecture, SBC Warburg, Swiss Bank House, London, England, January 11, 1996, transcript, Margaret Thatcher Foundation, http://www.margaretthatcher.org/document/108353.

36. Milton and Rose Friedman, *Free to Choose: A Personal Statement* (New York: Harcourt Brace and Company, 1980), 35.

37. Margaret Thatcher, "Speech at St Lawrence Jewry," London, England, March 4, 1981, transcript, Margaret Thatcher Foundation, http://www.margaretthatcher.org/document/104587.

38. Margaret Thatcher, "Dimensions of Conservatism," Iain Macleod Memorial Lecture, speech to Greater London Young Conservatives, Caxton Hall, London, England, July 4, 1977, transcript, Margaret Thatcher Foundation, http://www.margaretthatcher.org/document/103411. She continued, "It was an age of constant and constructive endeavour in which the desire to improve the lot of the ordinary person was a powerful factor. We who are largely living off the Victorians' moral and physical capital can hardly afford to denigrate them."

39. Margaret Thatcher, "Speech at Dinner to Lord Jakobivits (Retirement)," Grosvenor House Hotel, London, England, February 21, 1991, transcript, Margaret Thatcher Foundation, http://www.margaretthatcher.org/document/108261.

40. Thatcher, *The Path to Power*, 5.

41. Ibid., 11.

42. Margaret Thatcher, interview by David Frost, TV-AM, December 30, 1988.

43. Thatcher, *The Path to Power*, 5.

44. Ibid.

45. Margaret Thatcher, "Speech to Finchley Methodists (Education Sunday)," Finchley Methodist Church, Finchley, England, October 10, 1971, transcript, Margaret Thatcher Foundation, http://www.margaretthatcher.org/document/102140.

46. Margaret Thatcher, "I BELIEVE—A Speech on Christianity and Politics," speech at St. Lawrence Jewry, London, England, March 30, 1978, transcript, Margaret Thatcher Foundation, http://www.margaretthatcher.org/document/103522.

47. Ibid.

48. Ibid.

49. Thatcher, "Speech at St Lawrence Jewry," March 4, 1981.

50. Margaret Thatcher, "Speech to General Assembly of the Church of Scotland," Assembly Hall, Edinburgh, Scotland, May 21, 1988, transcript, Margaret Thatcher Foundation, http://www.margaretthatcher.org/document/107246.

51. Thatcher, "Speech Accepting an Honorary Degree from Hofstra University."

52. F. A. Hayek, *The Road to Serfdom* (Chicago: The University of Chicago Press, 1994), 63.

53. Ibid., 39.

54. Thatcher, *The Path to Power*, 21.

55. Thatcher, "Speech Accepting an Honorary Degree from Hofstra University."

56. Thatcher, *The Path to Power*, 50.

57. Ibid., 51.

58. Ibid., 50.

59. Walter Bagehot, *The English Constitution*, ed. Paul Smith (Cambridge: Cambridge University Press, 2001), 180.

60. Thatcher, *The Downing Street Years*, 687.

61. Ibid.

62. Thatcher, "Speech Accepting an Honorary Degree from Hofstra University."

63. Kenneth Harris, *Thatcher* (Boston: Little, Brown and Company, 1988), 49.

64. Thatcher, "Speech at St Lawrence Jewry," March 4, 1981.

65. F. A. Hayek, *The Constitution of Liberty: The Definitive Edition*, ed. Ronald Hamowy (Chicago: The University of Chicago Press, 2011), 455.

66. Thatcher, "Speech at St Lawrence Jewry," March 4, 1981.

67. Ruth Alexander, "Which Is the World's Biggest Employer?," *BBC News Magazine*, March 19, 2012, http://www.bbc.co.uk/news/magazine-17429786.

68. Alistair Horne, *Harold Macmillan*, vol. 2, *1957–1986* (New York: Viking Books, 1989), 64.

69. Ibid.

70. Thatcher, *The Path to Power*, 92.

71. Ibid., 50.

72. Ibid., 149.

73. Margaret Thatcher, "Speech to Conservative Rally in Cardiff," City Hall, Cardiff, England, April 16, 1979, transcript, Margaret Thatcher Foundation, http://www.margaretthatcher.org/document/104011.

74. Thatcher, "Speech Accepting an Honorary Degree from Hofstra University."

75. Ibid.

76. Ibid.

77. Ibid.

78. Ibid.

79. Ibid.

80. Margaret Thatcher, "Speech to Conservative Central Council," Kensington Town Hall, West London, England, March 26, 1983, transcript, Margaret Thatcher Foundation, http://www.margaretthatcher.org/document/105285.

81. Walter Isaacson, *Benjamin Franklin, An American Life* (New York: Simon and Schuster, 2003), 230.

82. Thatcher, *The Downing Street Years*, 753.

83. Ibid.

84. Ibid., 754.

85. Thatcher, "Speech Accepting an Honorary Degree from Hofstra University."

86. Thatcher, *The Downing Street Years*, 753.

87. Bagehot, *The English Constitution*, 180.

88. Margaret Thatcher, radio interview by Peter Spencer, IRN, July 16, 1989, transcript, Margaret Thatcher Foundation, http://www.margaretthatcher.org/document/107734.

89. Andrew Roberts, "The Genius of Thatcherism Will Endure," *Wall Street Journal*, April 8, 2013, http://online.wsj.com/article/SB10001424127887324050304578410692913779414.html.

Chapter 3

1. Margaret Thatcher, "Speech to Conservative Party Conference," Blackpool, England, October 10, 1975, transcript, Margaret Thatcher Foundation, http://www.margaretthatcher.org/document/102777.

2. Peter Riddell, *The Thatcher Era and Its Legacy* (Oxford, England: Blackwell, 1991), 37.

3. Ibid., 39.

4. Ibid., 41.

5. Ibid., 40.

6. Ibid.

7. James Denman and Paul McDonald, "Unemployment Statistics from 1881 to the Present Day," The Government Statistical Service (UK), Office for National Statistics (UK), http://www.ons.gov.uk/ons/rcl/lms/labour-market-trends—discontinued-/january-1996/unemployment-since-1881.pdf.

8. Ibid.

9. Sir Rhodes Boyson and Antonio Martino, "What We Can Learn from Margaret Thatcher," lecture no. 650, Heritage Foundation Windsor Society, Sea Island, GA,

October 3–6, 1999, transcript, http://www.heritage.org/research/lecture/what-we-can-learn-from-margaret-thatcher.

10. "UK Inflation 1790-2005," Bank of England, http://www.bankofengland.co.uk/education/Pages/inflation/timeline/chart.aspx.

11. Robert Twigger, "Inflation: The Value of the Pound 1750–1998," Research Paper 99/20, House of Commons Library, February 23, 1999, http://www.parliament.uk/documents/commons/lib/research/rp99/rp99-020.pdf.

12. "The Henderson Despatch (British Decline, Causes & Consequences) [leaked 1979; declassified 2006]," Sir Nicholas Henderson to David Owen, March 31, 1979, 5, http://www.margaretthatcher.org/archive/displaydocument.asp?docid=110961. The dispatch was released to the Margaret Thatcher Foundation in September 2006 after a FOIA request. It had originally been printed (nearly complete) in the *Economist* on June 2, 1979.

13. Ibid., 3.

14. Michael Barone, "What 1946 Can Tell Us About 2010," *American: The Online Magazine of the American Enterprise Institute*, April 6, 2010, http://www.american.com/archive/2010/april/what-1946-can-tell-us-about-2010.

15. Ibid.

16. Ibid.

17. Ibid.

18. John Maynard Keynes, *The General Theory of Employment, Interest and Money* (New York: Harcourt, Brace and Company, 1936), 381.

19. Margaret Thatcher, *The Path to Power* (New York: HarperCollins, 1995), 566.

20. Ibid.

21. Ibid.

22. Margaret Thatcher, "The Renewal of Britain," speech to the Conservative Political Centre Summer School, July 6, 1979, transcript, Margaret Thatcher Foundation, http://www.margaretthatcher.org/document/104107.

23. John Maynard Keynes, *Essays in Persuasion* (London: Rupert Hart-Davis, 1951), 312. Italics in original.

24. Keynes, *Essays in Persuasion*, 316.

25. John Kenneth Galbraith, "How Keynes Came to America," in *Essays on John Maynard Keynes*, ed. Milo Keynes (Cambridge: Cambridge University Press, 1975), 133.

26. Ibid., 138.

27. Edward Nelson and Kalin Nikolov, "Monetary Policy and Stagflation in the UK," Bank of England working paper #155 (2002), 8, http://www.bankofengland.co.uk/publications/Documents/workingpapers/wp155.pdf.

28. Paul A. Samuelson, *Economics*, 9th ed. (New York: McGraw-Hill Book Company, 1973), 827. Italics in original.

29. Ibid., 833.

30. Gene Healy, "Remembering Nixon's Wage and Price Controls," *Washington Examiner*, August 16, 2011. Reproduced on Cato.org, March 16, 2012, http://www.cato.org/publications/commentary/remembering-nixons-wage-price-controls.

31. Andrew Roberts, *A History of the English-Speaking Peoples Since 1900* (New York: HarperCollins, 2007), 490.

32. Ibid.

33. Thatcher, *The Path to Power*, 567–68.

34. Margaret Thatcher, "Statement on the Death of Milton Friedman," November 17, 2006, Margaret Thatcher Foundation, http://www.margaretthatcher.org/commentary/displaydocument.asp?docid=110883.

35. Margaret Thatcher, "Speech to the British Chambers of Commerce," Savoy Hotel, London, England, January 10, 1979, transcript, Margaret Thatcher Foundation, http://www.margaretthatcher.org/document/103922.

36. 720 Parl. Deb., H.C. (5th ser.) (1965) 1165. Also available online at *Hansard*, http://hansard.millbanksystems.com/commons/1965/nov/17/economic-affairs#S5CV0720P0_19651117_HOC_286%7Cpublisher=hansard%7Ctitle=%7Cdate=17.

37. Ibid.

38. Ibid.

39. Peter Jenkins, *Mrs. Thatcher's Revolution: The Ending of the Socialist Era* (Cambridge, Massachusetts: Harvard, 1988), 9.

40. Ibid. See also Riddell, *The Thatcher Era and Its Legacy*, 34.

41. "Why Does the 1970s Get Painted as Such a Bad Decade?" *BBC News Magazine*, April 15, 2012, http://www.bbc.co.uk/news/magazine-17703483.

42. Kit Dawnay, "A History of Sterling," *Daily Telegraph* (London), October 8, 2001, http://www.telegraph.co.uk/news/1399693/A-history-of-sterling.html.

43. Joe Moran, "Defining Moment: Denis Healey Agrees to the Demands of the IMF," *Financial Times*, September 4, 2010, http://www.ft.com/cms/s/2/11484844-b565-11df-9af8-00144feabdc0.html#axzz2OEjiZmpp.

44. Thatcher, *The Path to Power*, 320.

45. Samuelson, *Economics*, 825.

46. Dominic Sandbrook, *Seasons in the Sun: The Battle for Britain, 1974–1979* (London: Allen Lane, 2012), 715–19.

47. "UK Inflation 1790–2005."

48. Riddell, *The Thatcher Era and Its Legacy*, 50.

49. Kenneth Harris, *Thatcher* (Boston: Little, Brown, 1988), 73.
50. "Winter of Discontent Led Callaghan to Brink of Calling in the Army, 30-Year Papers Reveal," *Daily Mail* (UK), December 29, 2009, http://www.dailymail.co.uk/news/article-1239283/Winter-Discontent-led-Callaghan-brink-calling-Army.html#axzz2KBViV9oS.
51. Ibid.
52. Ibid.
53. Thatcher, *The Path to Power*, 425.
54. "'Crisis? What Crisis?,'" BBC News Online, September 12, 2000, http://news.bbc.co.uk/2/hi/uk_news/politics/921524.stm.
55. Nikki Brownlie, *Trade Union Membership 2011*, Department for Business Innovation and Skills (BIS) (UK), April 2012, https://www.gov.uk/government/uploads/system/uploads/attachment_data/file/16381/12-p77-trade-union-membership-2011.pdf.
56. Jenkins, *Mrs. Thatcher's Revolution*, 15.
57. "Obituary: Jack Jones," *Daily Telegraph* (UK), April 22, 2009, http://www.telegraph.co.uk/news/obituaries/politics-obituaries/5200632/Jack-Jones.html.
58. Thatcher, "Speech to British American Chamber of Commerce."

Chapter 4

1. Margaret Thatcher, "Don't Undo My Work," *Newsweek*, April 27, 1992, Margaret Thatcher Foundation, http://www.margaretthatcher.org/document/111359.
2. Margaret Thatcher, *The Path to Power* (New York: HarperCollins, 1995), 267.
3. Ibid., 181.
4. Margaret Thatcher, *The Downing Street Years* (New York: HarperCollins, 1993), 7.
5. Ibid.
6. Jock Bruce-Gardyne, *Mrs. Thatcher's First Administration: The Prophets Confounded* (London: Macmillan, 1984), 4.
7. Thatcher, *The Path to Power*, 269.
8. Ibid., 266.
9. Ibid., 267.
10. Margaret Thatcher, "My Kind of Tory Party," *Daily Telegraph*, January 30, 1975, Margaret Thatcher Foundation, http://www.margaretthatcher.org/document/102600.
11. Ibid. Italics in original.
12. Bruce-Gardyne, *Mrs. Thatcher's First Administration*, 4.

13. "Obituary: Jack Jones," *Daily Telegraph* (UK), April 22, 2009, http://www.telegraph. co.uk/news/obituaries/politics-obituaries/5200632/Jack-Jones.html.

14. Peter Jenkins, *Mrs. Thatcher's Revolution* (Cambridge, MA: Harvard University Press, 1988), 15, 158.

15. Ibid., 23.

16. Thatcher, *The Path to Power*, 424.

17. Ibid., 421.

18. Ibid., 430.

19. Kenneth Harris, *Thatcher* (Boston: Little, Brown, 1988), 74.

20. Margaret Thatcher, interview by Brian Walden, *Weekend World*, January 7, 1979, transcript, Margaret Thatcher Foundation, http://www.margaretthatcher.org/ document/103807.

21. Margaret Thatcher, "House of Commons Speech [Industrial Situation]," January 16, 1979, transcript, Margaret Thatcher Foundation, http://www.margaretthatcher. org/document/103924.

22. Ibid.

23. Margaret Thatcher, "Conservative Party Political Broadcast," TV broadcast from House of Commons, January 17, 1979, transcript, Margaret Thatcher Foundation, http://www.margaretthatcher.org/document/103926.

24. Ibid.

25. Thatcher, "House of Commons Speech [Industrial Situation]."

26. Ibid.

27. Thatcher, *The Path to Power*, 431.

28. Ibid., 433.

29. Margaret Thatcher, "Speech to Conservative Rally in Cardiff," City Hall, Cardiff, England, April 16, 1979, transcript, Margaret Thatcher Foundation, http://www. margaretthatcher.org/document/104011. She also repeated the line in her speech to a Conservative rally in Bolton on May 1, 1979, at http://www.margaretthatcher. org/document/104065; as well as in an abridged version of her speech in Finchley on May 2, 1979, at http://www.margaretthatcher.org/document/104072.

30. Margaret Thatcher, "Speech to Conservative Rally in Bolton," Bolton Town Hall, Lancashire, England, May 1, 1979, transcript, Margaret Thatcher Foundation, http://www.margaretthatcher.org/document/104065. The Tennyson quotation is from "Hands All Round": "That man's the true Conservative / Who lops the moulder'd branch away."

31. Margaret Thatcher, "Party Election Broadcast," Charlotte Street, Central London, April 30, 1979, transcript, Margaret Thatcher Foundation, http://www.margaret thatcher.org/document/104055.

32. Ibid.

33. William F. Buckley, "Margaret Is My Darling," *Athwart History: Half a Century of Polemics, Animadversions, and Illuminations* (New York: Encounter Books, 2010), 348. Italics in original.

34. Ibid., 349.

35. Ibid., 350.

36. Ibid., 348.

37. Mikhail Gorbachev, "The Margaret Thatcher I Knew," *Guardian* (UK), April 8, 2013, http://www.guardian.co.uk/politics/2013/apr/08/mikhail-gorbachev-margaret-thatcher-death. Italics added.

38. Thatcher, "Don't Undo My Work."

39. Thatcher, *The Downing Street Years*, 265.

40. Ibid.

41. "Margaret Thatcher & the Centre for Policy Studies, 1974–79," Margaret Thatcher Foundation, http://www.margaretthatcher.org/archive/CPS2.asp.

42. Peter B. Sperry, "The Real Reagan Economic Record: Responsible and Successful Fiscal Policy," *Backgrounder*, no. 1414, Heritage Foundation, March 1, 2001, http://www.heritage.org/research/reports/2001/03/the-real-reagan-economic-record.

43. Thatcher, *The Path to Power*, 575.

44. Ibid., 573.

45. Peter Riddell, *The Thatcher Era and Its Legacy* (Oxford: Blackwell, 1991), 27.

46. Thatcher, *The Path to Power*, 574.

47. Robin Harris, *Not For Turning: The Life of Margaret Thatcher* (London: Bantam Press, 2013), 225.

48. Riddell, *The Thatcher Era and Its Legacy*, 50. See also Thatcher, *The Path to Power*, 575.

49. Thatcher, *The Path to Power*, 575.

50. See Roger Scruton, "The Meaning of Margaret Thatcher," *Times* (UK), April 18, 2013, http://www.thetimes.co.uk/tto/news/uk/article3742279.ece.

51. Riddell, *The Thatcher Era and Its Legacy*, 50.

52. Thatcher, "Don't Undo My Work."

Chapter 5

1. Margaret Thatcher, *Statecraft: Strategies For A Changing World* (London: HarperCollins, 2002), 320.

2. Margaret Thatcher interview by Llew Gardner, *This Week*, February 5, 1976, transcript, Margaret Thatcher Foundation, http://www.margaretthatcher.org/document/102953.

3. Margaret Thatcher, "Speech to Conservative Central Council," West Midlands, England, March 24, 1979, transcript http://www.margaretthatcher.org/document/103980.

4. Ibid.

5. Ibid.

6. Margaret Thatcher, *The Downing Street Years* (London: HarperCollins, 1993), 63.

7. Sir Rhodes Boyson and Antonio Martino, "What We Can Learn from Margaret Thatcher," *Lecture*, no. 650, Heritage Foundation, November 24, 1999, http://www.heritage.org/research/lecture/what-we-can-learn-from-margaret-thatcher.

8. Quoted in Margaret Thatcher, *The Path to Power* (London: HarperCollins, 1995), 357.

9. Margaret Thatcher, "Speech to Conservative Party Conference," Brighton, England, October 10, 1980, transcript, Margaret Thatcher Foundation, http://www.margaretthatcher.org/document/104431.

10. Margaret Thatcher, "Speech at Kensington Town Hall," England, January 19, 1976, transcript, Margaret Thatcher Foundation, http://www.margaretthatcher.org/document/102939.

11. Margaret Thatcher, "Speech to Conservative Rally in Solihull," West Midlands, England, Margaret Thatcher Foundation, May 28, 1987, transcript, http://www.margaretthatcher.org/document/106852.

12. Margaret Thatcher, "Speech at Fleetwood," England, June 7, 1983, transcript, Margaret Thatcher Foundation, http://www.margaretthatcher.org/document/105385.

13. Margaret Thatcher, "The Principles of Thatcherism," speech, Seoul, South Korea, September 3, 1992, transcript, Margaret Thatcher Foundation, http://www.margaretthatcher.org/document/108302.

14. Boyson and Martino, "What We Can Learn from Margaret Thatcher."

15. Margaret Thatcher, "Speech to CNN World Economic Development Conference," Washington, D.C., September 19, 1992, transcript, Margaret Thatcher Foundation, http://www.margaretthatcher.org/document/108304.

16. Margaret Thatcher, "Dimensions of Conservatism," Iain Macleod Memorial Lecture, speech to Greater London Young Conservatives, London, England, July

4, 1977, transcript, Margaret Thatcher Foundation, http://www.margaretthatcher. org/document/103411.

17. "Americans Downbeat on State of U.S., Prospects for Future," Gallup, January 21, 2013, http://www.gallup.com/poll/160046/americans-downbeat-state-prospects-future.aspx.

18. "Obama's Fourth Year in Office Ties as Most Polarized Ever," Gallup, January 24, 2013, http://www.gallup.com/poll/160097/obama-fourth-year-office-ties-polarized-ever.aspx.

19. Rachel Cooper, "China 'to Overtake America by 2016,'" *Daily Telegraph* (UK), March 22, 2013, http://www.telegraph.co.uk/finance/china-business/9947825/China-to-overtake-America-by-2016.html.

20. Nile Gardiner, "America Is Sinking under Obama's Towering Debt," *Daily Telegraph* (UK), July 2, 2010, http://blogs.telegraph.co.uk/news/nilegardiner/100045733/america-is-sinking-under-obama%E2%80%99s-towering-debt/.

21. Margaret Thatcher, "Don't Undo My Work," *Newsweek*, April 27, 1992, Margaret Thatcher Foundation, http://www.margaretthatcher.org/document/111359.

22. "Public Debt as a Percentage of GDP in Countries around the World," *Global Finance*, based on data as of December 2012, http://www.gfmag.com/component/content/article/119-economic-data/12370-public-debt-percentage-gdp.html#axzz2Wfkfv8v1.

23. Patrick Tyrrell and William W. Beach, "U.S. Government Increases National Debt—and Keeps 128 Million People on Government Programs," *Backgrounder*, no. 2756, Heritage Foundation, January 8, 2013, http://www.heritage.org/research/reports/2013/01/us-government-increases-national-debtand-keeps-128-million-people-on-government-programs.

24. "The 2012 Long-Term Budget Outlook," Congressional Budget Office, June 2012, http://www.cbo.gov/sites/default/files/cbofiles/attachments/06-05-Long-Term_Budget_Outlook_2.pdf.

25. Ibid.

26. Bob Moffit and Alyene Senger, "Obamacare Budget Bombshell," *Foundry*, blog, Heritage Foundation, February 26, 2013, http://blog.heritage.org/2013/02/26/obamacare-budget-bombshell/.

27. "Past the Cliff, but Not Out of the Woods: Long-Term Analysis of the American Taxpayer Relief Act of 2012," Peter G. Peterson Foundation, January 29, 2013, http://www.pgpf.org/Issues/Fiscal-Outlook/2013/01/fiscal-cliff-atra-2012-long-term-analysis.aspx.

28. "Federal Spending Grew Nearly 12 Times Faster Than Median Income," chart, "Federal Budget in Pictures: Budget Chart Book," Heritage Foundation, 2012, http://www.heritage.org/federalbudget/.

29. Margaret Thatcher, "Speech at National Press Club," Washington, D.C., June 26, 1995, transcript, Margaret Thatcher Foundation, http://www.margaretthatcher.org/document/108344.

30. "64 Percent Think Too Many Are Dependent On Government Aid," Rasmussen Reports, March 28, 2013, http://www.rasmussenreports.com/public_content/business/general_business/march_2013/64_think_too_many_are_dependent_on_government_aid.

31. "Americans Favor Work Over Welfare as Response to Poverty," Rasmussen Reports, March 29, 2013, http://www.rasmussenreports.com/public_content/business/general_business/march_2013/americans_favor_work_over_welfare_as_response_to_poverty.

32. "Budget Background: Federal Welfare Spending to Grow Almost 80% over the Next Ten Years," United States Senate, Committee on the Budget: Republicans, "Charts," January 15, 2013, http://www.budget.senate.gov/republican/public/index.cfm/budget-background?ID=ef8afb72-42ce-4576-9648-35d2cbae7e32.

33. "Budget Background: Total Welfare Spending Equates to $168 per Day for Every Household in Poverty," United States Senate, Committee on the Budget: Republicans, December 7, 2012, http://www.budget.senate.gov/republican/public/index.cfm/budget-background?ID=f1f23669-79fb-4a25-bafc-6a28f82f9c75.

34. Tyrrell and Beach, "U.S. Government Increases National Debt—and Keeps 128 Million People on Government Programs."

35. Ibid.

36. Phil Izzo, "Nearly 1 in 6 Americans Receives Food Stamps," *Wall Street Journal*, July 8, 2013, http://blogs.wsj.com/economics/2013/07/08/nearly-1-in-6-americans-receive-food-stamps/.

37. Margaret Thatcher, "The Principles of Conservatism," lecture to the Heritage Foundation, Washington, D.C., December 10, 1997, transcript, Margaret Thatcher Foundation, http://www.margaretthatcher.org/document/108376.

38. "President Obama's Second Inaugural Address (Transcript)," *Washington Post*, speech delivered on January 21, 2013, http://www.washingtonpost.com/politics/president-obamas-second-inaugural-address-transcript/2013/01/21/f148d234-63d6-11e2-85f5-a8a9228e55e7_story.html.

39. Thatcher, *Statecraft*, 331.

40. David Cameron, "Speech on the Future of Europe," London, January 23, 2013, transcript, http://www.number10.gov.uk/news/david-cameron-eu-speech/.

41. Rachel Cooper, "Eurozone to Stay in Recession for Another Year," *Daily Telegraph* (UK), February 22, 2013, http://www.telegraph.co.uk/finance/financialcrisis/9887537/Eurozone-to-stay-in-recession-for-another-year.html.

42. "Spain Unemployment Rate Hit a Record: Youth Rate at 55 Percent," BBC News Online, January 24, 2013, at http://www.bbc.co.uk/news/business-21180371.

43. "Favorables: Socialism 24%, Capitalism 68%," Rasmussen Reports, November 28, 2012, http://www.rasmussenreports.com/public_content/politics/general_politics/november_2012/favorables_socialism_24_capitalism_68.

44. "U.S. per Person Debt Now 35 Percent Higher Than That of Greece," United States Senate, Committee on the Budget: Republicans, "Charts," http://www.budget.senate.gov/republican/public/index.cfm/charts.

45. Ibid.

46. Ibid.

47. Nile Gardiner, "128 Million Americans Are Now on Government Programmes. Can America Survive as the World's Superpower?," *Telegraph Blogs* (UK), January 8, 2013, http://blogs.telegraph.co.uk/news/nilegardiner/100196709/128-million-americans-are-now-on-government-programs-can-america-survive-as-the-worlds-superpower/.

48. "U.S. to Add Three Times More Debt Than Eurozone Over 5 Years," United States Senate, Committee on the Budget: Republicans, "Charts," http://www.budget.senate.gov/republican/public/index.cfm/charts.

49. Daniel Hannan, *Why America Must Not Follow Europe*, Encounter Broadside No. 19, March 1, 2011.

50. Henry Samuel, "Francois Hollande, the Drab Socialist Who Declared Finance His 'True Enemy,'" *Daily Telegraph* (UK), April 22, 2012, http://www.telegraph.co.uk/news/worldnews/europe/france/9219689/Francois-Hollande-the-drab-Socialist-who-declared-finance-his-true-enemy.html.

51. Roland Oliphant, "Gerard Depardieu 'Building a Wooden House So He Can Go Fishing in Russia,'" *Daily Telegraph* (UK), January 18, 2013, http://www.telegraph.co.uk/news/celebritynews/9811764/Gerard-Depardieu-building-a-wooden-house-so-he-can-go-fishing-in-Russia.html.

52. Ambrose Evans-Pritchard, "French Capital Flight Spikes as Hollande Hits Business," *Daily Telegraph* (UK), January 13, 2013, http://www.telegraph.co.uk/finance/9798891/French-capital-flight-spikes-as-Hollande-hits-business.html.

53. Graham Ruddick, "France 'Totally Bankrupt', Says Labour Minister Michel Sapin," *Daily Telegraph* (UK), January 28, 2013, http://www.telegraph.co.uk/finance/financialcrisis/9832845/France-totally-bankrupt-says-labour-minister-Michel-Sapin.html.

54. Henry Samuel, "Defiant Francois Hollande Pledges Supertax on Companies," *Daily Telegraph* (UK), March 28, 2013, http://www.telegraph.co.uk/news/world-news/europe/france/9960907/Defiant-Francois-Hollande-pledges-supertax-on-companies.html.

55. Stephane Pedrazzi and Catherine Boyle, "French Socialist in Mittal Row: We're Just Doing What Obama Does," CNBC.com, November 30, 2012, http://www.cnbc.com/id/50022833/French_Socialist_in_Mittal_Row_We039re_Just_Doing_What_Obama_Does.

56. Angelique Chrisafis, "Francois Hollande Seeks to Reassure UK and City of London," *Guardian*, February 13, 2012, http://www.guardian.co.uk/world/2012/feb/17/francois-hollande-uk-city-london.

57. 2013 Index of Economic Freedom, Heritage Foundation/*Wall Street Journal*, http://www.heritage.org/index/ranking.

58. Margaret Thatcher, "Speech at Georgetown University," February 27, 1981, transcript, Margaret Thatcher Foundation, http://www.margaretthatcher.org/document/104580.

59. Margaret Thatcher, "Europe—the Obligations of Liberty," Winston Churchill Memorial Lecture, Luxembourg, transcript, Margaret Thatcher Foundation, October 18, 1979, http://www.margaretthatcher.org/document/104149.

60. Thatcher, "The Principles of Thatcherism."

61. Margaret Thatcher, "Speech to Conservative Rally at Cheltenham," England, July 3, 1982, transcript, Margaret Thatcher Foundation, http://www.margaretthatcher.org/document/104989.

62. "62% Favor Smaller Government with Fewer Services, Lower Taxes," Rasmussen Reports, January 26, 2013, http://www.rasmussenreports.com/public_content/archive/mood_of_america_archive/benchmarks/62_favor_smaller_government_with_fewer_services_lower_taxes.

63. Margaret Thatcher, "Speech to Conservative Party Conference," Blackpool, England, October 14, 1983, transcript, Margaret Thatcher Foundation, http://www.margaretthatcher.org/document/105454.

Chapter 6

1. Margaret Thatcher, "Speech to Conservative Party Conference," Bournemouth, England, October 12, 1990, transcript, Margaret Thatcher Foundation, http://www.margaretthatcher.org/document/108217.

2. Margaret Thatcher, "Speech Receiving Honorary Degree from the Mendeleyev Institute," Moscow, Russia, July 22, 1993, transcript, Margaret Thatcher Foundation, http://www.margaretthatcher.org/document/108318.

3.   Margaret Thatcher, "Speech at Jagiellonian University in Krakow," Poland, October 3, 1991, transcript, Margaret Thatcher Foundation, http://www.margaretthatcher.org/document/108284.

4.   Margaret Thatcher, "The Language of Liberty," speech to the English-Speaking Union in New York, December 7, 1999, transcript, Margaret Thatcher Foundation, http://www.margaretthatcher.org/document/108386.

5.   Margaret Thatcher, "A Leader for the Nineties," interview with Olivia O'Leary, Yorkshire TV, June 9, 1987, transcript, Margaret Thatcher Foundation, http://www.margaretthatcher.org/document/106881.

6.   Margaret Thatcher, "Speech at National Press Club (*The Path to Power*)," Washington, D.C., June 26, 1995, transcript, Margaret Thatcher Foundation, http://www.margaretthatcher.org/document/108344.

7.   Margaret Thatcher, "Speech at the 33rd Churchill Memorial Concert at Blenheim Palace," England, March 6, 1999, transcript, Margaret Thatcher Foundation, http://www.margaretthatcher.org/document/108380.

8.   Margaret Thatcher, "Managing Conflict—The Role of International Intervention," speech to the Aspen Institute, Colorado, August 4, 1995, transcript, Margaret Thatcher Foundation, http://www.margaretthatcher.org/document/108346.

9.   "Transcript of Obama's Message in Celebration of Nowruz," *Wall Street Journal*, March 20, 2009, http://online.wsj.com/article/SB123752091165792573.html.

10.   Scott Wilson, "Muted Response Reflects U.S. Diplomatic Dilemma," *Washington Post*, June 15, 2009, http://www.washingtonpost.com/wp-dyn/content/article/2009/06/14/AR2009061402684_pf.html.

11.   "Statement by Press Secretary Robert Gibbs on the Iranian Election," press release, The White House, June 13, 2009, http://www.whitehouse.gov/the-press-office/statement-press-secretary-robert-gibbs-iranian-election.

12.   Con Coughlin, "Obama's Iran Diplomacy Isn't Working," *Wall Street Journal*, November 10, 2009, http://online.wsj.com/article/SB10001424052748704402404574527261228630446.html.

13.   Barack Obama, "Responsibility for our Common Future," address to the United Nations General Assembly, September 23, 2009, transcript, United States Mission to the United Nations, http://usun.state.gov/briefing/statements/2009/september/129519.htm.

14.   See Stephanie McCrummen, "U.S. Envoy's Outreach to Sudan is Criticized as Naïve," *Washington Post*, September 29, 2009, http://articles.washingtonpost.com/2009-09-29/world/36843338_1_bashir-president-omar-hassan-scott-gration.

15. Scott Wilson and Al Kamen, "'Global War on Terror' Is Given New Name," *Washington Post*, March 25, 2009, http://www.washingtonpost.com/wp-dyn/content/article/2009/03/24/AR2009032402818_pf.html.

16. Joe Biden, "Remarks by Vice President Biden at 45th Munich Conference on Security Policy," February 7, 2009, transcript, The White House, http://www.whitehouse.gov/the-press-office/remarks-vice-president-biden-45th-munich-conference-security-policy.

17. "An Open Letter to the Obama Administration from Central and Eastern Europe," *Gazeta Wyborcza*, July 15, 2009, http://wyborcza.pl/1,76842,6825987,An_Open_Letter_to_the_Obama_Administration_from_Central.html.

18. Edwin Meese III and Richard Perle, "New START: What Would Reagan Do?," *Wall Street Journal*, December 2, 2010, http://online.wsj.com/article/SB100014240527487046792045756471835061494438.html.

19. Jake Tapper, "President Obama Asks Medvedev for 'Space' on Missile Defense—'After My Election I Have More Flexibility,'" Political Punch Blog, *ABC News Online*, March 26, 2012, http://abcnews.go.com/blogs/politics/2012/03/president-obama-asks-medvedev-for-space-on-missile-defense-after-my-election-i-have-more-flexibility/.

20. "Interview with President Dmitry Medvedev," *Financial Times*, transcript, June 19, 2011, http://www.ft.com/intl/cms/s/0/4bfa1f38-9a90-11e0-bab2-00144feab49a.html.

21. Margaret Thatcher, "A Time for Leadership," speech to the Hoover Institution, California, July 19, 2000, transcript, Margaret Thatcher Foundation, http://www.margaretthatcher.org/document/108388.

22. Thatcher, "Speech Receiving Honorary Degree from the Mendeleyev Institute."

23. See Margaret Thatcher, "Speech Accepting the Morgenthau Award," New York, October 1, 1990, transcript, Margaret Thatcher Foundation, http://www.margaretthatcher.org/document/108209.

24. Thatcher, "Speech Accepting the Morgenthau Award."

25. Thatcher, "Speech at the 33rd Churchill Memorial Concert at Blenheim Palace."

26. Thatcher, "Speech Accepting the Morgenthau Award."

27. Margaret Thatcher, "Britain Awake (The Iron Lady)," speech at Kensington Town Hall, January 19, 1976, transcript, Margaret Thatcher Foundation, http://www.margaretthatcher.org/document/102939.

28. Margaret Thatcher, "First Clare Boothe Luce Lecture," Washington, D.C., September 23, 1991, transcript, Margaret Thatcher Foundation, http://www.margaretthatcher.org/document/108282.

29. Robin Harris, "We Abandon Christians in the East at Our Peril," *Standpoint*, April 2013, http://standpointmag.co.uk/node/4905/full.

30. Margaret Thatcher, "The Principles of Thatcherism," speech, Seoul, South Korea, September 3, 1992, transcript, Margaret Thatcher Foundation, http://www.margaretthatcher.org/document/108302.

31. Thatcher, "Britain Awake."

32. Ibid.

33. Ibid.

34. Ibid.

35. Ibid.

36. Margaret Thatcher, "Speech to Conservative Rally at Cheltenham," England, July 3, 1982, transcript, Margaret Thatcher Foundation, http://www.margaretthatcher.org/document/104989.

37. Margaret Thatcher, *The Downing Street Years* (London: HarperCollins, 1993), 238.

38. Margaret Thatcher, "The Defence of Freedom," speech accepting the Donovan Award, New York, February 28, 1981, transcript, Margaret Thatcher Foundation, http://www.margaretthatcher.org/document/104584.

39. Margaret Thatcher, "Speech to Conservative Women's Conference," London, May 22, 1985, transcript, Margaret Thatcher Foundation, http://www.margaretthatcher.org/document/106056.

40. Margaret Thatcher, "General Election Press Conference," Smith Square, London, England, May 25, 1983, transcript, Margaret Thatcher Foundation, http://www.margaretthatcher.org/document/105336.

41. Margaret Thatcher, interview by Geoffrey Smith, *Times* (UK), March 24, 1986, transcript, Margaret Thatcher Foundation, http://www.margaretthatcher.org/document/106206.

42. Thatcher, "A Time for Leadership."

43. Margaret Thatcher, "Speech to Conservative Rally in Newport," England, May 26, 1987, transcript, Margaret Thatcher Foundation, http://www.margaretthatcher.org/document/106843.

44. Margaret Thatcher, "Speech to Conservative Rally in Solihull," West Midlands, England, May 28, 1987, transcript, Margaret Thatcher Foundation, http://www.margaretthatcher.org/document/106852.

45. Margaret Thatcher, "Speech to Chelsea Conservative Association," London, England, July 26, 1975, transcript, Margaret Thatcher Foundation, http://www.margaretthatcher.org/document/102750.

46. See for example Margaret Thatcher, "Speech to a Conservative Rally," Dorking, Surrey, England, July 31, 1976, transcript, Margaret Thatcher Foundation, http://www.margaretthatcher.org/document/103086.

47. Margaret Thatcher, "The Sinews of Foreign Policy," speech to Les Grandes Conferences Catholiques, Brussels, Belgium, June 23, 1978, transcript, Margaret Thatcher Foundation, http://www.margaretthatcher.org/document/103720.

48. Thatcher, "Speech to a Conservative Rally."

49. "Prime Minister's Questions," House of Commons, June 5, 1980, transcript, Margaret Thatcher Foundation, http://www.margaretthatcher.org/document/104374.

50. Margaret Thatcher, "Speech at Lord Mayor's Banquet," Guildhall, London, November 10, 1986, transcript, Margaret Thatcher Foundation, http://www.margaretthatcher.org/document/106512.

51. Margaret Thatcher, interview by Michael Jones, *Sunday Times*, February 21, 1990, transcript, Margaret Thatcher Foundation, http://www.margaretthatcher.org/document/107865.

52. Margaret Thatcher, *Statecraft: Strategies For A Changing World* (London: HarperCollins, 1995), 15.

53. Thatcher, "Speech Accepting the Morgenthau Award."

54. Thatcher, "First Clare Boothe Luce Lecture."

55. See Margaret Thatcher, "Speech to the Winston Churchill Foundation Award Dinner," British Embassy, Washington, D.C., September 29, 1983, transcript, Margaret Thatcher Foundation, http://www.margaretthatcher.org/document/105450.

56. Margaret Thatcher, "Europe as I See It," speech, Rome, Italy, June 24, 1977, transcript, Margaret Thatcher Foundation, http://www.margaretthatcher.org/document/103403.

57. Thatcher, *The Downing Street Years*, 456.

58. Ibid., 485.

59. Margaret Thatcher, "TV Interview for Soviet Television," March 31, 1987, transcript, Margaret Thatcher Foundation, http://www.margaretthatcher.org/document/106604.

60. Thatcher, *The Downing Street Years*, 479.

61. Ibid., 780–782.

62. Margaret Thatcher, "Speech to Supreme Soviet of the USSR," Moscow, May 28, 1991, transcript, Margaret Thatcher Foundation, http://www.margaretthatcher.org/document/108272.

63. Thatcher, *The Downing Street Years*, 452.

64. Margaret Thatcher, interview by David Frost, TV-AM, December 30, 1988, transcript, Margaret Thatcher Foundation, http://www.margaretthatcher.org/document/107022.

65. Thatcher, *The Downing Street Years*, 463.

66. Margaret Thatcher, interview by John Cole, BBC, December 17, 1984, transcript, Margaret Thatcher Foundation, http://www.margaretthatcher.org/document/105592.

67. Margaret Thatcher, "Remarks on the Berlin Wall (Fall thereof)," London, England, November 10, 1989, transcript, Margaret Thatcher Foundation, http://www.margaretthatcher.org/document/107819.

68. Margaret Thatcher, "Speech to Conservative Central Council," Torquay, March 21, 1987, transcript, Margaret Thatcher Foundation, http://www.margaretthatcher.org/document/106769.

69. Thatcher, *The Downing Street Years*, 463.

70. Thatcher, *Statecraft*, 11.

71. Ibid., 7.

72. Margaret Thatcher, "Speech Receiving Medal of Freedom Award," Washington, D.C., March 7, 1991, transcript, Margaret Thatcher Foundation, http://www.margaretthatcher.org/document/108263.

73. Thatcher, "Speech to Conservative Party Conference," Bournemouth, England, October 12, 1990.

74. Quoted by Margaret Thatcher, "Speech to the 25th Annual UN Ambassadors Dinner," New York, September 24, 1991, transcript, Margaret Thatcher Foundation, http://www.margaretthatcher.org/document/108283.

75. Thatcher, "The Defence of Freedom."

Chapter 7

1. Margaret Thatcher, "Speech to Conservative Rally at Cheltenham," England, July 3, 1982, transcript, Margaret Thatcher Foundation, http://www.margaretthatcher.org/document/104989.

2. Ibid.

3. Margaret Thatcher, *The Downing Street Years* (London: HarperCollins, 1993), 181.

4. Ibid., 173.

5. Margaret Thatcher, "Speech at the *Salute to the Task Force* Lunch," Guildhall, City of London, October 12, 1982, transcript, Margaret Thatcher Foundation, http://www.margaretthatcher.org/document/105034.

6.   For more background on the history of the Falklands, see Luke Coffey, Theodore R. Bromund, and Nile Gardiner, "The United States Should Recognize British Sovereignty over the Falkland Islands," *Backgrounder*, no. 2771, Heritage Foundation, March 4, 2013, http://www.heritage.org/research/reports/2013/03/the-united-states-should-recognize-british-sovereignty-over-the-falkland-islands.

7.   Margaret Thatcher, "Speech on Board the *Canberra*," April 8, 1997, transcript, Margaret Thatcher Foundation, http://www.margaretthatcher.org/document/108370.

8.   Margaret Thatcher, "Speech to Conservative Women's Conference," London, May 26, 1982, transcript, Margaret Thatcher Foundation, http://www.margaretthatcher.org/document/104948.

9.   Margaret Thatcher, interview by British Forces Broadcasting Service, June 10, 1982, transcript, Margaret Thatcher Foundation, http://www.margaretthatcher.org/document/104962.

10.   Thatcher, *The Downing Street Years*, 179.

11.   Michael Jopling memo to Frances Pym, April 6, 1982, Margaret Thatcher Foundation, http://www.margaretthatcher.org/document/B4192C197DE04F68B9CC724BE42A4664.pdf.

12.   Margaret Thatcher statement to the House of Commons, April 3, 1982, transcript, Margaret Thatcher Foundation, http://www.margaretthatcher.org/document/104910.

13.   Margaret Thatcher, "Speech at the *Salute to the Task Force* Lunch."

14.   Peter Foster, "Margaret Thatcher and the Falklands War: Doubts and Fears in a Far-Off Conflict That Changed Britain," *Daily Telegraph* (UK), April 8, 2013, http://www.telegraph.co.uk/news/politics/margaret-thatcher/9980046/Margaret-Thatcher-and-the-Falklands-War-doubts-and-fears-in-a-far-off-conflict-that-changed-Britain.html.

15.   Margaret Thatcher, "Fortune *Does*, in the End, Favour the Brave," message on the twenty-fifth anniversary of the liberation of the Falklands, June 13, 2007, transcript, Margaret Thatcher Foundation, http://www.margaretthatcher.org/document/110962.

16.   Thatcher, "Speech on Board the *Canberra*."

17.   Ibid.

18.   Margaret Thatcher, "Speech at the 33rd Churchill Memorial Concert at Blenheim Palace," March 6, 1999, transcript, Margaret Thatcher Foundation, http://www.margaretthatcher.org/document/108380.

19.   Margaret Thatcher, interview by David Frost, TV-AM, June 7, 1985, transcript, Margaret Thatcher Foundation, http://www.margaretthatcher.org/document/ 105826.

20.   Thatcher, *The Downing Street Years*, 213.

21.   Ibid., 182–83.

22.   Ibid., 227.

23.   Ibid., 173.

24.   Ibid., 188.

25.   Ronald Reagan, interview by Western European Television Correspondents, Paris, June 1, 1982, transcript, University of Texas, Ronald Reagan Presidential Library, http://www.reagan.utexas.edu/archives/speeches/1982/ 60182d.htm.

26.   "Remarks Following Talks with President Reagan," London, England, June 9, 1982, transcript, http://www.margaretthatcher.org/document/104961.

27.   Thatcher, "Speech to Conservative Rally at Cheltenham."

28.   Thatcher, *The Downing Street Years*, 174.

29.   Thatcher, "Speech to Conservative Rally at Cheltenham."

Chapter 8

1.   Margaret Thatcher, "Fortune *Does*, in the End, Favour the Brave," message on the twenty-fifth anniversary of the liberation of the Falklands, June 13, 2007, transcript, Margaret Thatcher Foundation, http://www.margaretthatcher.org/ document/110962.

2.   Margaret Thatcher, *The Downing Street Years* (London: HarperCollins, 1993), 237.

3.   Margaret Thatcher, "Speech to Joint Houses of Congress," Washington, D.C., February 20, 1985, transcript, http://www.margaretthatcher.org/document/105968.

4.   Margaret Thatcher, "The New World Order," speech to the Fraser Institute, Toronto, November 8, 1993, transcript, Margaret Thatcher Foundation, http:// www.margaretthatcher.org/document/108325.

5.   Luke Coffey, "NATO: The Chicago Summit and U.S. Foreign Policy," testimony before the Committee on Foreign Affairs' Subcommittee on Europe and Eurasia, United States House of Representatives, April 27, 2012, transcript, Heritage Foundation, http://www.heritage.org/research/testimony/2012/04/nato-the- chicago-summit-and-us-foreign-policy.

6.   Robert M. Gates, "The Security and Defense Agenda (Future of NATO)," Brussels, Belgium, June 10, 2011, transcript, United States Department of Defense, http:// www.defense.gov/speeches/speech.aspx?speechid=1581.

7. Margaret Thatcher, "Speech to the National Press Club," Washington, D.C., November 5, 1993, transcript, Margaret Thatcher Foundation, http://www.margaretthatcher.org/document/108324.

8. Cole Moreton, "Falkland Islands: Britain 'Would Lose' if Argentina Decides to Invade Now," *Daily Telegraph* (UK), March 17, 2012, http://www.telegraph.co.uk/news/worldnews/southamerica/falklandislands/9150339/Falkland-Islands-Britain-would-lose-if-Argentina-decides-to-invade-now.html.

9. Damien McElroy, "Falklands 'Will Be under Our Control in 20 Years', Says Argentine Foreign Minister," *Daily Telegraph* (UK), February 5, 2013, http://www.telegraph.co.uk/news/worldnews/southamerica/falklandislands/9849971/Falklands-will-be-under-our-control-in-20-years-says-Argentine-foreign-minister.html.

10. Cole Moreton, "Britain Faces 'Impossible' Battle if Argentina Invades Falklands, Warns General Sir Mike Jackson," *Daily Telegraph* (UK), January 29, 2012, http://www.telegraph.co.uk/news/worldnews/southamerica/falklandislands/9046476/Britain-faces-impossible-battle-if-Argentina-invades-Falklands-warns-General-Sir-Michael-Jackson.html.

11. "Warning: Hollow Force Ahead! The Effect of Ever More Defense Budget Cuts on U.S. Armed Forces," Defending Defense Project, the American Enterprise Institute, the Heritage Foundation, and the Foreign Policy Initiative, July 2011, http://www.heritage.org/research/reports/2011/07/defending-defense-warning-hollow-force-ahead.

12. Mackenzie Eaglen, "Defense Cuts and America's Outdated Military," *Wall Street Journal*, January 24, 2012, http://online.wsj.com/article/SB10001424052970203806504577179322078800612.html.

13. *An American Century: A Strategy to Secure America's Enduring Interests and Ideals*: A Romney for President White Paper, October 7, 2011, http://www.scribd.com/doc/67928028/An-American-Century%E2%80%94A-Strategy-to-Secure-America%E2%80%99s-Enduring-Interests-and-Ideals.

14. "Warning: Hollow Force Ahead!"

15. See Mackenzie Eaglen and Julia Pollak, "U.S. Military Technological Supremacy under Threat," American Enterprise Institute, November 28, 2012, http://www.aei.org/papers/foreign-and-defense-policy/defense/us-military-technological-supremacy-under-threat/.

16. See Luke Coffey, "Keeping America Safe: Why U.S. Bases in Europe Remain Vital," *Special Report*, no. 111, Heritage Foundation, July 11, 2012, http://www.heritage.org/research/reports/2012/07/keeping-america-safe-why-us-bases-in-europe-remain-vital.

17. Coffey, "Keeping America Safe."

18. Margaret Thatcher, "Speech to Conservative Party Conference," Brighton, England, October 8, 1982, transcript, Margaret Thatcher Foundation, http://www.margaretthatcher.org/document/105032.

19. Margaret Thatcher, "Speech at Fleetwood," Fleetwood, England, June 7, 1983, transcript, Margaret Thatcher Foundation, http://www.margaretthatcher.org/document/105385.

20. Quoted by Margaret Thatcher, "Speech to the General Assembly of the Commonwealth of Virginia," Richmond, February 3, 1995, transcript, Margaret Thatcher Foundation, http://www.margaretthatcher.org/document/108342.

21. Margaret Thatcher, "Speech to the North Atlantic Assembly," November 17, 1982, transcript, Margaret Thatcher Foundation, http://www.margaretthatcher.org/document/105056.

22. Margaret Thatcher, "Speech to Conservative Central Council," West Midlands, England, March 24, 1979, transcript, Margaret Thatcher Foundation, http://www.margaretthatcher.org/document/103980.

23. Margaret Thatcher, "Speech at Conservative Party Conference," Blackpool, England, October 16, 1981, transcript, Margaret Thatcher Foundation, http://www.margaretthatcher.org/document/104717.

24. Margaret Thatcher, "Speech to Joint Houses of Congress."

25. Thatcher, *The Downing Street Years*, 89.

26. Ibid., 379–80.

27. Robin Harris, "Thatcher Knew How to Fight Terrorists," *Daily Telegraph* (UK), October 13, 2004, http://www.telegraph.co.uk/comment/personal-view/3611957/Thatcher-knew-how-to-fight-terrorists.html.

28. Thatcher, "Speech to Conservative Party Conference," Brighton, England, October 12, 1984.

29. Thatcher, *The Downing Street Years*, 397.

30. Margaret Thatcher, "Speech at Lord Mayor's Banquet," London, November 16, 1987, transcript, http://www.margaretthatcher.org/document/106965.

31. Thatcher, *The Downing Street Years*, 414.

32. Margaret Thatcher, "The West Must Prevail," remarks accepting the Clare Boothe Luce Award, Heritage Foundation, Washington, D.C., December 9, 2002, transcript, Margaret Thatcher Foundation, http://www.margaretthatcher.org/document/110687.

33. Margaret Thatcher, "Advice to a Superpower," *New York Times*, February 11, 2002, http://www.nytimes.com/2002/02/11/opinion/advice-to-a-superpower.html?src=pm.

34. Con Coughlin, "Al-Qaeda Threat: Britain Worst in Western World," *Daily Telegraph* (UK), January 15, 2010, http://www.telegraph.co.uk/news/uknews/terrorism-in-the-uk/6996655/Al-Qaeda-threat-Britain-worst-in-western-world.html.

35. Theodore R. Bromund and Morgan L. Roach, "Islamist Terrorist Plots in Great Britain: Uncovering the Global Network," *Backgrounder*, no. 2329, Heritage Foundation, October 26, 2009, http://www.heritage.org/research/reports/2009/10/islamist-terrorist-plots-in-great-britain-uncovering-the-global-network.

36. Tom Whitehead, "Suicide Bomb Gang Guilty of Plotting 'Worst Ever Terror Attack in Britain,'" *Daily Telegraph* (UK), February 21, 2013, http://www.telegraph.co.uk/news/uknews/terrorism-in-the-uk/9877193/Suicide-bomb-gang-guilty-of-plotting-worst-ever-terror-attack-in-Britain.html.

37. James Jay Carafano, Steve Bucci, and Jessica Zuckerman, "Fifty Terror Plots Foiled Since 9/11: The Homegrown Threat and the Long War on Terrorism," *Backgrounder*, no. 2682, Heritage Foundation April 25, 2012, http://www.heritage.org/research/reports/2012/04/fifty-terror-plots-foiled-since-9-11-the-homegrown-threat-and-the-long-war-on-terrorism.

38. See James Jay Carafano and Paul Rosenzweig, *Winning the Long War: Lessons from the Cold War for Defeating Terrorism and Preserving Freedom* (Washington, D.C.: Heritage Books, 2005).

39. Margaret Thatcher, "Speech to Conservative Party Conference," Brighton, England, October 12, 1984.

Chapter 9

1. Margaret Thatcher, "Shaping a New Global Community," speech to the Aspen Institute, Aspen, Colorado, August 5, 1990, transcript, Margaret Thatcher Foundation, http://www.margaretthatcher.org/document/108174.

2. Quoted by Ronald Reagan at a White House State banquet for Margaret Thatcher, Washington, D.C., November 16, 1988, transcript, Margaret Thatcher Foundation, http://www.margaretthatcher.org/document/107384.

3. Margaret Thatcher, *Statecraft: Strategies For A Changing World* (London: HarperCollins, 1995), 20.

4. Margaret Thatcher, interview by David Frost, TV-AM, December 30, 1988, transcript, Margaret Thatcher Foundation, http://www.margaretthatcher.org/document/107022.

5. Margaret Thatcher, "Speech to the Los Angeles World Affairs Council," November 16, 1991, transcript, Margaret Thatcher Foundation, http://www.margaretthatcher.org/document/108290.

6.   Ibid.

7.   Margaret Thatcher, "Speech to the National Press Club," Washington, D.C., November 5, 1993, transcript, Margaret Thatcher Foundation, http://www. margaretthatcher.org/document/108324.

8.   Margaret Thatcher, "Speech at the 33rd Churchill Memorial Concert at Blenheim Palace," March 6, 1999, transcript, Margaret Thatcher Foundation, http://www. margaretthatcher.org/document/108380.

9.   Margaret Thatcher, "The Language of Liberty," speech to the English-Speaking Union in New York, December 7, 1999, transcript, Margaret Thatcher Foundation, http://www.margaretthatcher.org/document/108386.

10.   "U.S. Visit: State Department Program for Margaret Thatcher's 1967 U.S. Tour (20 February–31 March 1967)," State Department records, available at the Margaret Thatcher Foundation, http://www.margaretthatcher.org/archive/display-document.asp?docid=109473.

11.   Margaret Thatcher, *The Path to Power* (London: HarperCollins, 1995), 360.

12.   Margaret Thatcher, "Speech to the National Press Club," Washington, D.C., September 19, 1975, transcript, Margaret Thatcher Foundation, http://www. margaretthatcher.org/document/102770.

13.   Margaret Thatcher, "Speech at White House Arrival Ceremony," December 17, 1979, transcript, Margaret Thatcher Foundation, http://www.margaretthatcher. org/document/104194.

14.   Margaret Thatcher, "The Principles of Conservatism," lecture to the Heritage Foundation, Washington, D.C., December 10, 1997, transcript, Margaret Thatcher Foundation, http://www.margaretthatcher.org/document/108376.

15.   Margaret Thatcher, *The Downing Street Years* (London: HarperCollins, 1993), 69.

16.   John O'Sullivan, *The President, the Pope, and the Prime Minister: Three Who Changed the World* (Washington, D.C.: Regnery, 2006), 138.

17.   Margaret Thatcher, "Remarks Arriving at the White House," February 26, 1981, transcript, http://www.margaretthatcher.org/document/104576.

18.   Margaret Thatcher and Ronald Reagan, exchange of toasts at White House Dinner, February 26, 1981, transcript, Margaret Thatcher Foundation, http://www. margaretthatcher.org/document/104579.

19.   Margaret Thatcher and Ronald Reagan, exchange of toasts at British Embassy Dinner, Washington, D.C., February 27, 1981, transcript, Margaret Thatcher Foundation, http://www.margaretthatcher.org/document/104581.

20.   Ronald Reagan, *An American Life: The Autobiography* (New York: Simon & Schuster, 1990), 204.

21. Ibid.

22. Thatcher, *The Path to Power*, 372.

23. Thatcher, *The Downing Street Years*, 157.

24. Fred Emery, "Letter to President-Elect Reagan (Invitation to Visit Britain)," *Times* (UK), November 6, 1980, Margaret Thatcher Foundation, http://www.margaretthatcher.org/document/104216.

25. Margaret Thatcher, "Letter to President-Elect Reagan," January 20, 1981, http://www.margaretthatcher.org/document/104553.

26. Margaret Thatcher, "Reagan's Leadership, America's Recovery," *National Review*, December 30, 1988, http://www.nationalreview.com/articles/258884/reagan-s-leadership-america-s-recovery-margaret-thatcher.

27. Margaret Thatcher, "Speech at National Press Club (*The Path to Power*)," Washington, D.C., June 26, 1995, transcript, Margaret Thatcher Foundation, http://www.margaretthatcher.org/document/108344.

28. Margaret Thatcher, interview by Leslie Stahl, CBS *Face the Nation*, Washington, D.C., July 17, 1987, transcript, Margaret Thatcher Foundation, http://www.margaretthatcher.org/document/106915.

29. Thatcher, *The Downing Street Years*, 771.

30. Margaret Thatcher and Ronald Reagan, "Speeches at White House Arrival Ceremony," November 16, 1988, transcript, Margaret Thatcher Foundation, http://www.margaretthatcher.org/document/107381.

31. Thatcher, *The Downing Street Years*, 446.

32. "Prime Minister's Questions," House of Commons, April 15, 1986, transcript, Margaret Thatcher Foundation, http://www.margaretthatcher.org/document/106361.

33. Margaret Thatcher, "House of Commons Statement: U.S. Bombing of Libya," April 15, 1986, transcript, Margaret Thatcher Foundation, http://www.margaretthatcher.org/document/106362.

34. Ibid.

35. Ibid.

36. Thatcher, *The Downing Street Years*, 449.

37. Ronald Reagan, interview by foreign journalists, Washington, D.C., April 22, 1986, transcript, University of Texas, Ronald Reagan Presidential Library, http://www.reagan.utexas.edu/archives/speeches/1986/42286h.htm.

38. Thatcher's meeting with George H. W. Bush is described in Thatcher, *The Downing Street Years*, 817.

39. Press conference with Margaret Thatcher and President George H. W. Bush, Aspen, Colorado, August 2, 1990, transcript, Margaret Thatcher Foundation, http://www.margaretthatcher.org/document/108170.

40. Thatcher, "Shaping a New Global Community."

41. Margaret Thatcher, "Speech at Dinner to Lord Jakobivits (Retirement)," Grosvenor Hall, London, February 21, 1991, transcript, Margaret Thatcher Foundation, http://www.margaretthatcher.org/document/108261.

42. Margaret Thatcher, interview by David Frost, TV-AM *Frost on Sunday*, September 1, 1990, transcript, Margaret Thatcher Foundation, http://www.margaretthatcher.org/document/108186.

43. Thatcher, *The Downing Street Years*, 820.

44. Ibid., 768–69.

45. The conversation is described by George H. W. Bush when he awarded Thatcher the Presidential Medal of Freedom on March 7, 1991.

46. Thatcher, *The Downing Street Years*, 821.

47. Thatcher, "Speech to the Los Angeles World Affairs Council."

48. Thatcher, "Speech to the National Press Club," November 5, 1993.

49. Margaret Thatcher, "Speech Receiving Medal of Freedom Award," Washington, D.C., March 7, 1991, transcript, Margaret Thatcher Foundation, http://www.margaretthatcher.org/document/108263.

50. Margaret Thatcher, "The West Must Prevail," remarks accepting Clare Boothe Luce Award, Heritage Foundation, Washington, D.C., December 9, 2002, transcript, Margaret Thatcher Foundation, http://www.margaretthatcher.org/document/110687.

51. Tony Blair, "Statement on Baroness Thatcher," April 8, 2013, http://www.tonyblairoffice.org/news/entry/statement-on-baroness-thatcher/.

52. Tim Shipman, "Barack Obama 'Too Tired' to Give Proper Welcome to Gordon Brown," *Sunday Telegraph* (UK), March 7, 2009, http://www.telegraph.co.uk/news/worldnews/barackobama/4953523/Barack-Obama-too-tired-to-give-proper-welcome-to-Gordon-Brown.html.

53. Tim Shipman, "France Is Our Biggest Ally, Declares Obama: President's Blow to Special Relationship with Britain," *Daily Mail* (UK), January 11, 2011, http://www.dailymail.co.uk/news/article-1346006/Barack-Obama-declares-France-biggest-ally-blow-Special-Relationship-Britain.html.

54. Nicholas Cecil, "Boris Johnson Tells Barack Obama: Stop Bashing Britain," *London Evening Standard*, June 10, 2010, http://www.standard.co.uk/news/boris-johnson-tells-barack-obama-stop-bashing-britain-6479222.html.

55. Hillary Clinton, "Remarks with Argentine President Cristina Fernandez de Kirchner," Buenos Aires, March 1, 2010, transcript, United States Department of State, http://www.state.gov/secretary/rm/2010/03/137539.htm.

56. Margaret Thatcher, "The Sinews of Foreign Policy," speech to Les Grandes Conferences Catholiques, Brussels, Belgium, June 23, 1978, transcript, Margaret Thatcher Foundation, http://www.margaretthatcher.org/document/103720.

57. "Remarks by President Obama at Strasbourg Town Hall," April 3, 2009, transcript, White House, http://www.whitehouse.gov/the-press-office/remarks-president-obama-strasbourg-town-hall.

58. "A New Beginning," remarks by President Barack Obama, Cairo University, Egypt, June 4, 2009, transcript, White House, http://www.whitehouse.gov/the-press-office/remarks-president-cairo-university-6-04-09.

59. "Obama's Interview with *Al Arabiya*," January 27, 2009, transcript, http://www.alarabiya.net/articles/2009/01/27/65096.html.

60. "Remarks by President Obama at the Summit of the Americas Opening Ceremony," Port of Spain, Trinidad and Tobago, April 18, 2009, transcript, White House, http://www.whitehouse.gov/the_press_office/Remarks-by-the-President-at-the-Summit-of-the-Americas-Opening-Ceremony/.

61. "Remarks by President Obama to the Turkish Parliament," Ankara, Turkey, April 6, 2009, transcript, White House, http://www.whitehouse.gov/the_press_office/Remarks-By-President-Obama-To-The-Turkish-Parliament/.

62. Margaret Thatcher, "Speech at the Winston Churchill Award Dinner," Washington, D.C., September 29, 1983, transcript, Margaret Thatcher Foundation, http://www.margaretthatcher.org/document/105450.

63. 2013 Index of Economic Freedom, Heritage Foundation/*Wall Street Journal*, http://www.heritage.org/index/ranking.

64. Andrew Roberts, *A History of the English-Speaking Peoples Since 1900* (New York: HarperCollins, 2007), 637.

65. Margaret Thatcher, "Speech to the National Press Club," November 5, 1993.

66. Margaret Thatcher, "Speech to the Winston Churchill Foundation Award Dinner."

67. Margaret Thatcher, "Speech to Joint Houses of Congress," Washington, D.C., February 20, 1985, transcript, Margaret Thatcher Foundation, http://www.margaretthatcher.org/document/105968.

68. Thatcher, "The Principles of Conservatism."

Chapter 10

1. Quoted in George Gale, "Nation on the Outside," *Daily Express*, October 17, 1981, Margaret Thatcher Foundation, http://www.margaretthatcher.org/document/ 104717.

2. Margaret Thatcher, "Speech to Conservative Women's Conference," Westminster, England, May 24, 1989, transcript, Margaret Thatcher Foundation, http://www. margaretthatcher.org/document/107675.

3. "Prime Minister's Questions," House of Commons, May 9, 1989, transcript, Margaret Thatcher Foundation, http://www.margaretthatcher.org/document/ 107661.

4. Margaret Thatcher, "Speech to Conservative Party Conference," Blackpool, England, October 12, 1979, transcript, Margaret Thatcher Foundation, http:// www.margaretthatcher.org/document/104147.

5. Margaret Thatcher, "Speech at the 33rd Churchill Memorial Concert at Blenheim Palace," March 6, 1999, transcript, Margaret Thatcher Foundation, http://www. margaretthatcher.org/document/108380.

6. Margaret Thatcher, "Speech to General Assembly of the Church of Scotland," May 21, 1988, transcript, Margaret Thatcher Foundation, http://www.margaretthatcher. org/document/107246.

7. Margaret Thatcher, "Speech to Conservative Central Council," West Midlands, England, March 24, 1979, transcript, http://www.margaretthatcher.org/document/ 103980.

8. Margaret Thatcher, "How I Couple Duties of M.P. and Mother," *Liverpool Daily Post*, December 6, 1960, Margaret Thatcher Foundation, http://www. margaretthatcher.org/document/100954.

9. Margaret Thatcher, interview by Brian Walden, *Weekend World*, January 16, 1983, transcript, Margaret Thatcher Foundation, http://www.margaretthatcher.org/ document/105087.

10. Ibid.

11. Margaret Thatcher, "Speech at Monash University (1981 Sir Robert Menzies Lecture)," October 6, 1981, Melbourne, transcript, Margaret Thatcher Foundation, http://www.margaretthatcher.org/document/104712.

12. Peter Dominiczak, "David Cameron: I Am Not a Thatcherite," *Daily Telegraph* (UK), April 28, 2013, http://www.telegraph.co.uk/news/politics/david-cameron/10023612/David-Cameron-I-am-not-a-Thatcherite.html.

13. Margaret Thatcher, "Speech at Lord Mayor's Banquet," London, England, November 10, 1980, transcript, Margaret Thatcher Foundation, http://www. margaretthatcher.org/document/104442.

14. Margaret Thatcher, "Speech to Conservative Party Conference," Blackpool, England, October 9, 1987, transcript, Margaret Thatcher Foundation, http://www.margaretthatcher.org/document/106941.

15. Margaret Thatcher, "The Reason Why," speech to Conservative Party Conference, Brighton, England, October 10, 1980, transcript, Margaret Thatcher Foundation, http://www.margaretthatcher.org/document/104431.

16. Margaret Thatcher, "Speech to Finchley Conservatives (10th Anniversary Party)," Hendon, England, April 21, 1989, transcript, Margaret Thatcher Foundation, http://www.margaretthatcher.org/document/107645.

17. Sir Rhodes Boyson and Antonio Martino, "What We Can Learn from Margaret Thatcher," *Lecture*, no. 650, Heritage Foundation, November 24, 1999, http://www.heritage.org/research/lecture/what-we-can-learn-from-margaret-thatcher.

18. Thatcher, "Speech to Conservative Party Conference," October 12, 1979.

19. Margaret Thatcher, "Speech to Conservative Party Conference," Blackpool, England, October 11, 1985, transcript, http://www.margaretthatcher.org/document/106145.

20. Margaret Thatcher and Ronald Reagan, exchange of Toasts at British Embassy Dinner, Washington, D.C., February 27, 1981, transcript, Margaret Thatcher Foundation, http://www.margaretthatcher.org/document/104581.

21. Quoted by Robin Harris, "Thatcher Knew How to Fight Terrorists," *Daily Telegraph* (UK), October 13, 2004, http://www.telegraph.co.uk/comment/personal-view/3611957/Thatcher-knew-how-to-fight-terrorists.html.

22. Margaret Thatcher, "Speech to Federation of Business and Professional Women (Golden Jubilee)," London, England, November 19, 1988, transcript, Margaret Thatcher Foundation, http://www.margaretthatcher.org/document/107391.

23. Thatcher, "Speech to Finchley Conservatives."

24. Margaret Thatcher, "Eulogy for President Reagan," delivered in Washington, D.C., via video link, June 11, 2004, transcript, Margaret Thatcher Foundation, http://www.margaretthatcher.org/document/110360.

25. Margaret Thatcher, "Press Conference in Washington," Washington, D.C., November 17, 1988, transcript, Margaret Thatcher Foundation, http://www.margaretthatcher.org/document/107386.

26. Margaret Thatcher, TV interview for Soviet television, Moscow, March 31, 1987, transcript, http://www.margaretthatcher.org/document/106604.

27. Thatcher, "How I Couple Duties of MP and Mother."

28. Margaret Thatcher, interview by David Frost, December 30, 1988, transcript, Margaret Thatcher Foundation, http://www.margaretthatcher.org/document/107022.

29.   Thatcher, "The Reason Why."

30.   Margaret Thatcher, "Britain Awake (The Iron Lady)," speech at Kensington Town Hall, England, January 19, 1976, transcript, Margaret Thatcher Foundation, http://www.margaretthatcher.org/document/102939.

31.   Margaret Thatcher, "The Bruges Speech," speech to the College of Europe, Bruges, September 20, 1988, transcript, Margaret Thatcher Foundation, http://www.margaretthatcher.org/document/107332.

32.   David Cameron, "EU Speech at Bloomberg," London, January 23, 2013, transcript, http://www.number10.gov.uk/news/eu-speech-at-bloomberg/.

33.   Margaret Thatcher, "The New Renaissance," speech to the Zurich Economic Society, Switzerland, March 14, 1977, transcript, Margaret Thatcher Foundation, http://www.margaretthatcher.org/document/103336.

34.   Rudyard Kipling, "The Dawn Wind," quoted in Thatcher, "The New Renaissance."

Conclusion

1.   Margaret Thatcher, "Don't Undo My Work," *Newsweek*, April 27, 1992, Margaret Thatcher Foundation, http://www.margaretthatcher.org/document/111359.

2.   Margaret Thatcher, interview with David Frost, TV-AM, December 30, 1988, transcript, Margaret Thatcher Foundation, http://www.margaretthatcher.org/document/107022.

3.   Toby Harnden, "Obama Campaign Defends His Comments to Voters to 'Get Revenge,'" *Daily Mail* (UK), November 3, 2012, http://www.dailymail.co.uk/news/article-2227421/Obama-campaign-defends-comment-voters-revenge-saying-response-Republican-lies-people-losing-jobs.html.

4.   Margaret Thatcher, "Speech at Conservative Party Conference," Blackpool, England, October 16, 1981, transcript, Margaret Thatcher Foundation, http://www.margaretthatcher.org/document/104717.

5.   Margaret Thatcher, "Europe—The Obligations of Liberty," Winston Churchill Memorial Lecture, Luxembourg, October 18, 1979, transcript, Margaret Thatcher Foundation, http://www.margaretthatcher.org/document/104149.

6.   Newt Gingrich, interview for "Commanding Heights," PBS, Spring 2001, transcript, http://www.pbs.org/wgbh/commandingheights/shared/minitextlo/int_newtgingrich.html.

7.   Ronald Reagan, *The Reagan Diaries* (New York: HarperCollins, 2007), 32.

8.   Margaret Thatcher, "Speech to the First International Conservative Congress," Washington, D.C., September 28, 1997, transcript, Margaret Thatcher Foundation, http://www.margaretthatcher.org/document/108374.

9.   Margaret Thatcher, "Speech to North Dallas Chamber of Commerce," Dallas, TX, March 11, 1991, transcript, Margaret Thatcher Foundation, http://www.margaretthatcher.org/document/108265.

10.   Margaret Thatcher, "Speech Paying Tribute to Ronald Reagan," March 1, 2002, transcript, Margaret Thatcher Foundation, http://www.margaretthatcher.org/document/109306.

11.   Thatcher, "Speech to the First International Conservative Congress."

12.   Ibid.

13.   Margaret Thatcher, "Don't Undo My Work."

14.   Ted Cruz, "What the GOP Should Stand For: Opportunity," *Washington Post*, January 3, 2013, http://articles.washingtonpost.com/2013-01-03/opinions/36210969_1_republican-policies-obama-policies-economic-policies.

15.   Thatcher, "Speech to the First International Conservative Congress."

16.   Ibid.

INDEX